IN THE NAME
OF JESUS

Receiving Power from the
Prayers of the New Testament

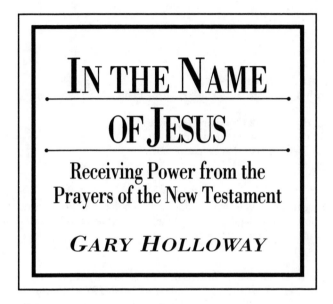

IN THE NAME
OF JESUS

Receiving Power from the
Prayers of the New Testament

GARY HOLLOWAY

— *A* —
FAITH*FOCUS*
Book

Sweet Publishing

Fort Worth, Texas

IN THE NAME OF JESUS
Receiving Power from the Prayers of the New Testament

Copyright © 1994 by Gary Holloway
Published by Sweet Publishing
3950 Fossil Creek Blvd., Suite 201
Fort Worth, TX 76137

Any royalties from this book are dedicated to the Institute for Christian Studies, Austin, Texas.

Cover: Gary Schecter for the Mustang Group

Library of Congress Catalog Number 94-65920

ISBN: 0-8344-0235-1

Printed in the U. S. A.
10 9 8 7 6 5 4 3 2 1

To Lem and Jean Rogers,
who gave me their daughter
as an answer to prayer.

Contents

PRAYERS OF PAUL

PRAYERS OF FAITH AND DISCIPLINE

INTRODUCTION

There are two extreme approaches to swimming. You can learn all about swimming, memorize the different strokes and practice in front of a mirror. You can read the stirring biographies of great Olympic swimmers who overcame their fear of the water to become great champions. You can become an expert on all the trivia of swimming, knowing every world record by heart.

When you finish all that, you still can't swim.

On the other hand, your dad could just throw you in the water. The theory is you'll sink or you'll swim.

But even if you come up treading water, that doesn't necessarily mean you can swim.

It's the same way with prayer. We can learn all *about* prayer and still not pray. We learn to pray only by praying. On the other hand, we must not think that the way we've always prayed is necessarily all that prayer can be.

What we need is an instructor, someone who'll teach us to pray, like a good swim coach will teach us to swim. We need someone to get down into the water with us, to hold us up when we need it, to let us go when we can begin to stay afloat.

Actually, we do have an instructor. Our prayer coach is Jesus. With patience and persistence he shows us how to pray—not just through his teachings, but also through his own prayers and those of the early Christians.

I still feel I have a lot more to learn about prayer. I continue learning by studying biblical examples of prayer, but primarily I'm learning through time spent in prayer.

This book is an invitation for you to learn with me. Together we will learn to pray from the One who understands us, who understands prayer, who understands God the most. As we study the prayers of the New Testament—all prayed by Jesus or prayed with Jesus—we can learn how Jesus prayed. We, too, can pray in the name of Jesus. But we can also learn to pray with Jesus.

This book explores what the New Testament says about prayer. Not every passage that mentions prayer is included, but every major prayer text is here. Learning with Jesus will help you examine and change your prayer life. I encourage you not only to read but to reflect. Not only to reflect, but to pray. And if you pray with Jesus, your life will be changed.

If you want to pray more and pray differently, you can use this book in a variety of ways. You can read it privately, with another Christian, in a small-group Bible study, or in a class at church. However you read it, my prayer is that this book will help you rediscover devotion to prayer and learn what Jesus and the early church knew: true power comes only through prayer.

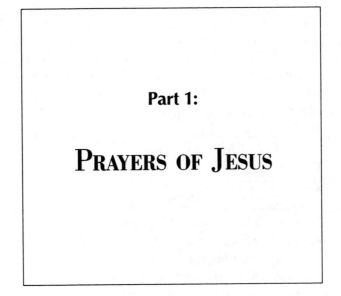

Part 1:

PRAYERS OF JESUS

Pray then in this way:
Our Father in heaven,
    hallowed be your name.
Your kingdom come.
Your will be done,
    on earth as it is in heaven.
Give us this day our daily bread.
And forgive us our debts,
    as we also have forgiven our debtors.
And do not bring us to the time of trial,
    but rescue us from the evil one.

Matthew 6:9-13 (NRSV)

Chapter 1

Lord,

Teach Me to Pray

$\mathcal{M}$y prayer life changed when I was eleven and my mother got cancer.

Prayer Focus:

Pray like Jesus.

Yes, I had always prayed. Some of my earliest memories are of prayer: "God is great, God is good" at the dinner table and "Now I lay me down to sleep" at night (usually followed by a long list, "God bless Mommy and Daddy and Suzy, our dog," and any others I could think of). My childhood prayers, like most, were rituals, sometimes meaningful, sometimes not.

But when my mother was diagnosed with cancer, an almost certain death sentence in those days, I suddenly didn't know how to pray. Should I pray for her to be healed? I certainly did. I prayed with all my might. That is, until it was clear she would not recover. Should I pray for her suffering to cease? She was in terrible pain, a pain that seeped through the morphine and other drugs in her body to disfigure her usually peaceful face. So I prayed for her relief.

My prayer was answered. Mom passed away in her sleep. I was devastated—how could I survive without my mother! But I continued to pray, not knowing what to ask for, not knowing how to cope.

And, again, God heard my prayer. He blessed me far above anything I could have ever imagined. My father remarried, and my second mother (I just call her "Mom") is as much a loving mother to me as my first one.

That experience changed my prayer life. No longer did I pray the rote prayers of childhood. No longer did I expect God's answers to always be simple or even pleasant. Other experiences of life have changed my prayers even more. How did I learn to pray? From my parents. From faithful Christians. From harsh experience.

Prayer. It's the source of power, but it's a source we have never really learned to tap for ourselves. How do you do it? Where do you begin? How do you know God is really listening? How do you hear his answers? How do you pray?

———❖———

It's midnight. There's a knock on the door. You stumble out of bed to find a policeman there. Your two sons have been in an accident. Both are dead.

How do you pray?

You go with your dad to the doctor. Dad is sixty-two and in good health, but lately he's been acting strange. The diagnosis: Alzheimer's disease.

How do you pray?

Another day begins. You get up at the same time, wash the same face, get in the same car, and go to the same job. You have a great family, a good career, a fine church. Life should be wonderful, but you feel empty inside.

How do you pray?

These are not hypothetical situations, but real ones. I know people who've been in each of these circumstances. So do you. Perhaps you're going through them yourself. When shocked, hurt, and confused, we know prayer can help. A recent *Life* magazine survey revealed that nine out of ten Americans pray frequently and earnestly—we're a nation that believes in prayer. But we sometimes can't bring ourselves to pray. We say we don't know how.

---

*Jesus himself teaches us the way,
if we will but slow down,
stand still, and hear his voice.*

I still don't really know how to pray. Although others help, there is one above all who teaches me to pray. His name is Jesus. He knew pain and loss, and he shares mine.

In times of pain we appreciate the plea of the first disciples, "Lord, teach us to pray" (Luke 11:1). Their cry is ours. For in every trial, when we usually learn the most, and in every joy in life, we can turn to God in prayer. Jesus himself teaches us the way, if we will but slow down, stand still, and hear his voice.

So how do you pray? You learn to pray like Jesus.

The Lord's Prayer

After his temptation and baptism, Jesus and his

disciples traveled throughout Galilee. As word about him spread, large crowds followed him. One day he went up on a mountainside and sat down to teach. In this "Sermon on the Mount" he took the opportunity to teach his followers about prayer.

His prayer, known as the "Lord's Prayer," the "Our Father," or the "Model Prayer," is also recorded in Luke 11:1-4 as Jesus' answer to the disciples' request, "Lord, teach us to pray." By whatever name, it is certainly the best known prayer among Christians and until recent years was known by practically everyone in the Western world.

So what new thing can be said about the Lord's Prayer? Dozens of books have been written on these few words. Any study of prayer in the New Testament has to start here, but since we know these words so well, what more can we learn from them?

By taking a fresh look at the familiar phrases of this prayer, perhaps we can recover some of its power and realize anew why this model prayer has stood the test of time.

Our Father in heaven. In this short address we see the great paradox of the nature of God. He is our Father. He is near; he is close to us. He gently cares for us. He knows all our needs. At the same time he is in heaven. He is God, not human. He is the all-powerful ruler of the universe. He is holy. His ways are not our ways. We cannot understand or control him. By calling God our Father in heaven, we come to him boldly, as we would to our own father, but we also bow face down before him, unworthy to lift our eyes to his glory.

Wayne is a friend of mine who preaches near Chicago. Once he decided to do something different in the worship service. The sermon text for that day was the story of Moses at the burning bush. Wayne

had someone read the part of Moses while he went to
the balcony to read the part of God. When they got to
that section in the passage where God speaks,
Wayne's booming voice rang out from the balcony,
"Moses, Moses, take off your shoes! . . ."

A little girl in the third row stood up in the pew
and asked in a loud voice, "Mommy, is that God?"
Then turning around to look at the balcony, she said
in an even louder voice, "Oh, it's just Wayne!"

"Our Father in heaven" reminds us that in
prayer, whatever we may think of ourselves, we are
just Wayne, or Gary, or Betty. God alone is the
Almighty One in heaven.

Hallowed be your name. We should hold this
great God in reverence. Though we draw close to
God in prayer, we bow before him, not only when we
pray, but symbolically in our whole life. Each moment we must show respect for God.

But there is more to this phrase than mere reverence for God. God reveals himself to us by his name.
Remember when Moses at the burning bush asked
the name of God, and God revealed it to him? So God
has more fully revealed his name and nature to us in
Christ. To pray that God will make his name holy is
to pray that he will reveal himself in our world.

Your kingdom come. This is the pivotal point of
the prayer. Jesus asks for the fulfillment of the
coming of the kingdom. For us to pray that God's
kingdom will come is to recognize that the kingdom
has already been inaugurated in the lives of the
church and that God's reign is increasing in the
present world. But the ultimate rule of God—God's
ultimate kingdom—will not be realized until the end
of time. We earnestly pray that God will reign, not
only at the end, but today in our lives.

Your will be done, on earth as it is in heaven.

For God to reign in our lives, we must be one with his will. This prayer has a cosmic significance. God's bidding is followed perfectly in heaven. We pray the day will come when it is followed perfectly on earth. But God's will also has a moral force in each Christian's life. If we want God's will to be done on earth, then it must begin with us—with me. Our will must be shaped to his. Like the angels in heaven, we must always stand prepared to do his will.

Give us this day our daily bread. This first of three requests seems straightforward. However, in Greek this is the most problematic phrase of the prayer. The word translated "daily" occurs only in the model prayer in the Greek New Testament. Scholars are not sure what it means. It may mean "daily bread." If so, it is right for us to ask God for the physical needs of life. Most modern Western Christians take daily food for granted. We need to be reminded that the necessities of life, even our meals, are a gift of God, not a natural right or something we have earned. "Daily" implies Christians should not hoard their resources, relying on their wealth instead of on God. God alone supplies our needs.

A good case can be made that the phrase should be translated "give us our bread for tomorrow." If so, God calls us to be farsighted. Planning for tomorrow is today's task. This doesn't mean we hoard our wealth or trust our plans instead of trusting God. It means God wants us to be wise in our actions. But Jesus also points us to the ultimate tomorrow, to the great messianic banquet to be enjoyed by his followers in the coming kingdom. So we pray not just for bread to fill our physical hunger, but more importantly, for "the bread of life"—Jesus himself.

Forgive us our debts, as we also have forgiven our debtors. Since we pray to "our Father in heaven," who is a holy God, we cannot pray without a sense of our own sin. We pray that our debts will be forgiven. Here sin is spoken of as a huge debt that we cannot repay, a theme Jesus repeats in the parable of the two debtors (Matthew 18:23-35). In this prayer, as in the parable, the enormity of the debt that God has forgiven prompts the disciple to forgive his debtors. The verb in "as we also _have forgiven_ our debtors" is significant. It does not mean that forgiving others earns our forgiveness, but that forgiveness of others should be such a feature of our lives that it is a given fact (see Matthew 6:14, 15).

And do not bring us to the time of trial, but rescue us from the evil one. The final request of the Lord's Prayer is for God's help in overcoming evil. Today, belief in Satan, the evil one, seems silly and superstitious to some. But the unbelievable degree of cruelty we see in the world and the inward knowledge of the depths of our own selfishness confirm what Jesus said: the evil one is close and powerful.

Though God is vastly more powerful than Satan, God's children are warned against overconfidence when facing evil. We ask God to keep us from the time of trial. The New Revised Standard Version renders a better translation than the familiar "Lead us not into temptation," since God tempts no one (James 1:13). God, however, does discipline those whom he loves and tests our faith to produce endurance (James 1:3). Knowing our own weaknesses, however, we must not ask for those tests. Instead, when Satan tempts or God tests our faith, it is the Father, not ourselves, whom we must trust for deliverance.

It may seem strange to ask God not to bring us to the time of trial. If he is a loving Father, surely he

will do nothing to harm us. That's true. He loves us
and will never hurt us. But we need to be reminded
of that fact.

This makes me think of Walt. Walt is a five year
old in our church who has amazing insights into
faith and prayer. When Walt was three he had a
painful operation on his leg. I helped his parents
take him to their car when he was dismissed from
the hospital. As his father gently lifted him into the
car, Walt said in a plaintive cry, "Don't hurt me,
Daddy." Patrick, Walt's father, would never hurt his
son, but Walt in his tender condition needed assurance. In the same way, we pray "keep us from evil."
Don't hurt me, Daddy.

The Kingdom Prayer

The Lord's Prayer is essentially a "kingdom
prayer"—a prayer for subjects in God's kingdom.
Our King in heaven is also our Father. We pray he
will continue to reveal himself on earth so all hu-
manity will reverence his name. We pray his rule
will grow on the earth, until that day when all here
serve him as completely as the angels in heaven do
now.

We recognize that in Christ the kingdom and rule
of God have already broken into our world, and we
pledge to live our lives under his rule. His kingdom
is here! But Satan's influence is still with us, so we
need God's power in our earthly walk. We pray for
our earthly bread, anticipating the heavenly feast.
We pray for forgiveness and the strength to forgive.
We pray for escape from trial and power to overcome
the evil one. And we pray for the day when he rules
over all—when every knee bows before him.

In this way the Lord's Prayer is a model for all
Christian prayer. We do more than simply pray

these words or make similar petitions to God. All our prayers are like the Lord's Prayer because we are citizens of his kingdom. All of our prayers must have this same sense of anticipation that the kingdom of this world has become, is becoming, and will become the kingdom of our Lord and Christ.

Recently I was overwhelmed at the power unleashed at the praying of the Lord's Prayer. I was preaching the funeral of Margaret, a devout Christian woman, one who gave freely of herself to others. The most touching moment of the service was not the hymns, the readings, or my own poor attempts at eloquence. No, the most comforting and uplifting moment was when the entire congregation spoke aloud the Lord's Prayer. Margaret had requested this for her funeral. Experiencing those words together brought those who loved her closer to each other and to God. We prayed these words with each other, but we also prayed them with Jesus—and he prayed them with us.

Let us thankfully join Jesus in approaching our heavenly Father with these familiar words—words taught us by his Son.

Focusing Your Faith:

1. If you can, recite the Lord's Prayer by heart. What is the value in memorizing this and other prayers in the Bible?

2. What importance did prayer play in your home as you were growing up?

3. How do you visualize God when you are talking to him?

4. How do you know God is really listening to your prayer? How do you listen to God?

5. What is the most difficult situation you have faced in prayer? How did God answer and help you?

6. In considering the phrase ". . . as we forgive," who is it in your life who needs your forgiveness? Have you really forgiven them?

7. Begin a prayer journal, recording your daily prayers. As Jesus teaches you to pray, look back at your prayers and see how he answers them.

Chapter 2

When We Ask,
He Still Teaches

$\mathcal{I}$n 1943 a group of American missionaries moved to the jungles of Bolivia to work with a tribe of Ayores. The fierce Ayores, seeing everyone outside their tribe as the enemy, brutally slaughtered five of the missionaries

Prayer Focus:

Pray with understanding.

as they entered the Indians' territory. The Ayores had not even given the missionaries a chance to greet them.

Even while grieving, the surviving missionaries continued to pray for and minister to these Indians. Their commitment, even to the point of death, must have impressed the Ayores. The missionaries regularly left gifts for them and slowly gained their trust. Finally they persuaded the Ayores to come out of the jungle to meet with them. Because of these

missionaries' commitment and love for those who
should have been their enemies, many Ayores were
later converted to Christ. The American missionaries certainly understood the phrase, "Love your
enemies." But they went beyond understanding it—
they practiced it.

Jesus Teaches the Disciples

In the Gospels Jesus teaches his followers many
things that seemed at the time to be counter to the
existing religious laws and practices.

Jesus warned his disciples that they must take
care that their righteousness exceeded that of the
scribes and Pharisees, the "holy men" of that day
(Matthew 5:20). In Matthew 6, Jesus explains what
that higher righteousness means in terms of outward acts of worship: giving, praying, and fasting.
Jesus certainly commends these acts of righteousness or piety, but to go beyond the practices of the
Pharisees, he teaches his disciples to do these acts
out of love for God, not for the praise of other people
and not just out of obedience.

Even before Jesus prays the Lord's Prayer, he
instructs his followers to pray what is for me the
most difficult prayer of all: prayer for our enemies.

> You have heard that it was said, "Love your
> neighbor and hate your enemy." But I tell you:
> Love your enemies and pray for those who perse-
> cute you, that you may be sons of your Father in
> heaven. He causes his sun to rise on the evil and
> the good, and sends rain on the righteous and the
> unrighteous. If you love those who love you, what
> reward will you get? Are not even the tax collec-
> tors doing that? And if you greet only your broth-
> ers, what are you doing more than others? Do not

even pagans do that? Be perfect, therefore, as your
heavenly Father is perfect (Matthew 5:43-48).

This call to higher righteousness goes beyond that
of the scribes and Pharisees. In the Old Testament,
an Israelite was to treat a fellow Israelite differently
than he would a stranger. The psalmist could pray
that his enemies would be completely and violently
destroyed. But Jesus calls his disciples back to the
nature of God himself: He cares for the righteous and
unrighteous, so we, too, must learn to love even our
enemies.

But surely good Christians have no enemies! So
we may think, until reality kicks us in the teeth. Has
someone at work smirked and rolled his eyes every
time you mention God or the church or answered
prayer? Have you ever been hassled for no reason by
some petty bureaucrat? Have friends ever deceived
you? Have they spread lies behind your back? Has a
loved one abandoned, abused, or neglected you? Has
someone caused the death of someone you love?

For several years I taught junior high in a Christian school. On one occasion my wife Deb asked Eric,
one of my seventh graders, what he thought of me
and my class. It so happened that I had gotten on to
Eric pretty severely the day before. "I wish he'd die,"
he told Deb. Somewhat taken aback, Deb reminded
him that was not a very Christian attitude. "OK,"
recanted Eric, "I just wish he'd fall off a mountain
and break his leg."

We may laugh at Eric's honesty, but I wonder if
there are adults who feel the same way about us but
won't admit it. Sometimes through no fault of our
own we make enemies. We shouldn't be surprised.
Jesus had them too. They did more than wish he'd
die, they killed him.

So what can it mean to love our enemies? Surely we can't have warm feelings toward someone who is doing everything in his power to destroy us. Jesus explains what this love means and what prayer means by adding, "pray for those who persecute you." We cannot *feel* good about someone who is inflicting pain on us unjustly. But we can *will* his good—we can desire that God will bless, not bring harm to such a person. Such blessing does not mean God accepts them as they are; we should pray for their repentance.

Love for the enemy does not necessarily turn one into a friend. We might pray for our persecutors and find they persecute us more severely. No matter. We still are to pray for them, because such prayer reflects the nature of the God who loved us while we were enemies (Romans 5:10).

> *With Jesus and the power of prayer, our feelings will change because our hearts will change.*

But how can such a prayer be sincere? Do we naturally have a heartfelt concern for the well-being of one who cheats us, calls us names, harasses us, jails us, yes, who even wants to kill us? No. It is natural to want revenge against our enemies. But the command of Jesus and the nature of our Father run counter to our feelings. Prayer is effective even when we don't feel like praying. Jesus teaches, "In spite of your righteous indignation, pray for the good of your persecutor." But how can we do that? We can't alone. With Jesus and the power of prayer, our feelings will change because our hearts will change.

The God who loathes our sins still loves us. Jesus himself helps us further understand this principle when he teaches us in this prayer as he was dying on the cross, "Father forgive them. . . ."

Jesus' Warnings

After Jesus teaches his audience about righteousness, he gives two warnings on prayer.

And when you pray, do not be like the hypocrites, for they love to pray standing in the synagogues and on the street corners to be seen by men. I tell you the truth, they have received their reward in full. But when you pray, go into your room, close the door and pray to your Father, who is unseen. Then your Father, who sees what is done in secret, will reward you. And when you pray, do not keep on babbling like pagans, for they think they will be heard because of their many words. Do not be like them, for your Father knows what you need before you ask him (Matthew 6:5-8).

Don't Be Showy

First he warns against praying publicly to be seen by others. The higher righteousness to which Christians are called is, first of all, not "showy." As with giving (Matthew 6:2-4), Jesus calls those who pray to be seen by others *hypocrites*. This is the Greek term for "actor," that is, someone who is playing a role. The implication here is that the hypocrites may not be completely insincere; they may truly believe in God and may be sincerely praying to him. The problem is, they are not praying to him *alone*. Like actors they are aware of their audience, of those in the synagogue or streets who hear them. Because it is this audience that they primarily wish to please, they have already received their reward. The approval or applause of those around them is the only answer their prayers will get. So they may think they are praying to God, but in truth they have another audience.

Once I was eating in the home of some friends. They asked their four-year-old daughter to say the blessing, but she spoke so softly that none of us could hear what she was saying. "Speak louder," her father said. "We can't hear you." She looked up from her prayer and said, "I wasn't talking to you, Daddy."

Jesus says to have an audience of one.

Jesus says to have an audience of one. "Go to your room, close the door, and pray to your Father in secret." The word translated "room" here is literally the "storeroom," the locked room in the house where valuables are kept. To pray in the storeroom is the exact opposite of praying on the street corner; here care is taken that no one but God will hear your prayer. If God alone is the audience for our prayers, then his applause is all we hear. More importantly, it is he who hears our prayers and he alone who can and will answer.

This command to pray alone is not a condemnation of all public or group prayer. Many Scriptures speak of the importance of prayer in public worship and the power of praying with our brothers and sisters. The Lord's Prayer itself addressed God as *our* Father, implying that it was a group prayer.

However, there is a strong warning here about public prayer. When leading prayer or voicing the prayer for a group, we certainly must consider the thoughts and feelings of those around us. We are praying *with* them, but we must never forget that we are all praying *to* God. It is God alone we address. It is God alone who answers prayer. And it is God alone who gives our reward.

Don't Babble

Having warned his disciples against praying like hypocrites, Jesus next warns them about praying like pagans.

Repeated prayers and persistence in prayer are not condemned here; Jesus himself commends these in other passages (Luke 18:1). Neither does he condemn the use of model or written prayers, since he gives them a model prayer, the Lord's Prayer, immediately following his warning. What Jesus condemns is a "magical" view of prayer. To many pagans, prayers were like magical incantations. What mattered to them was not the relationship between worshipers and their gods, but the repetition of the right phrases. As the saying goes, they were doing the thing right, and not doing the right thing.

To Jesus, these types of prayers were complete nonsense. If such prayers are worthless to a pagan god, how much more are they an affront to the living God? Scripture clearly says humans should not attempt to manipulate God. He is the sovereign Lord of the universe—not some tyrant who withholds his blessings until we ask. Nor is he a weak God who cannot bless until he hears the "magic words." This is the very view that Jesus opposes. He is a loving God who wants to bless, who knows what we need before we ask, yet who works in such a way that our will and our prayers somehow cooperate with his will in accomplishing his purposes for our lives.

Do we sometimes babble empty phrases? Do we simply repeat the prayer lines we have heard all our lives without thinking of what we say? Think about: "Guard, guide, and direct our ways." "Bless this food to our nourishment, and our bodies into thy service." "If we've been found faithful, may we have a home in heaven with Thee." All of these are prayer phrases from my youth. More recently, I hear a great many "just want'as" in prayer: "We just want'a thank you." You can probably make your own list of prayer phrases that are overused. This doesn't mean those who use them are guilty of babbling, but we must guard against using the "right words" in prayer without saying them from the heart.

In light of Jesus' words about empty babbling, it is ironic that his model prayer, the Lord's Prayer, has been repeated countless times in the history of Christianity. Perhaps our casual familiarity and rote way of repeating it have robbed us of the full power Jesus provides for us with this dynamic prayer.

Jesus' Lessons

Many of the lessons about prayer that Jesus taught his disciples were taught through miracles and parables of faith which were linked with prayer.

Expectant Faith

Jesus gives two examples in Mark concerning the role of faith in the power of prayer. In Mark 9, a father has a son with an evil spirit who throws the boy into the lake and into the fire. The boy's very life is in danger. The father brings his son to the disciples, but they cannot cast out the spirit. Their inability leads the father to doubt Jesus:

> "It has often thrown him into fire or water to kill him. But if you can do anything, take pity on us and help us."

> " 'If you can'?" said Jesus. "Everything is possible for him who believes."

> Immediately the boy's father exclaimed, "I do believe; help me overcome my unbelief!" (Mark 9:22-24).

Jesus then casts out the demon. His lesson on prayer is found in his reply to the disciples' question: "After Jesus had gone indoors, his disciples asked him privately, 'Why couldn't we drive it out?' He replied, 'This kind can come out only by prayer' " (Mark 9:28, 29).

This is a strange reply. By saying *"this kind* can come out only by prayer," is he suggesting that some demons can be cast out without the power of God? I don't think so. He implies that the disciples had too much confidence in their own power and not enough faith in the power of God.

There is an important lesson here for modern Christians. Too many times we live our lives like those around us, relying on our own abilities and actions—common sense, psychology, self-help, technology, prosperity—to solve our problems. Like these disciples, we may neglect to pray, or if we do pray, we turn to God as a last resort when "this kind" of problem—one we can't solve on our own—arises. This lack of faith is not what Jesus is recommending. True faith calls for us to rely totally on God through prayer at all times.

This story of a father, his child, and a fire reminds

me of another story. When my wife Deb was nine,
she and her family went tent camping in Colorado.
During the night, their gas lantern exploded, engulf-
ing their tent in flames. All made it outside all right
—or so they thought. But in the smoke and confusion they had lost sight of Deb's seven-year-old
sister, Gwen. The tent burned down around her. She
was severely burned. Everyone—even the doctors—
feared she would die.

Christians from all over the country rallied
around Gwen, sending her cards and flowers. The
First Lady, Lady Bird Johnson, even sent flowers.
More importantly, all joined in prayer for Gwen. She
was burned so seriously that she could not recover
on her own. It took fasting and prayer. During the
worst part of her ordeal, a visitor to the hospital
asked Gwen how she was doing. She cheerfully
replied, "I'm doing fine because I'm taking my medi-
cine, and everybody's praying for me."

By God's grace, Gwen survived. She now lives
with her husband Rush and her children Katie and
Sabre in Asheville, North Carolina. Gwen's been
through countless operations and many hours of
therapy, but there is no one on the earth who is
more gentle and loving and kind. Whenever I, like
the father in Mark, am tempted to doubt the power
of Jesus and the power of prayer, I have only to
think of Gwen and smile. It's Jesus' way of helping
my unbelief.

An explanation of faith and the power of prayer is
even more forcefully illustrated in Mark 11. Here,
also, Jesus' teaching on prayer is in the context of a
miracle. The day before, he had cursed a barren fig
tree (Mark 11:12-14). The next morning, the tree is
withered to its roots. This startles the disciples:

Peter remembered and said to Jesus, "Rabbi, look! The fig tree you cursed has withered!" "Have faith in God," Jesus answered. "I tell you the truth, if anyone says to this mountain, 'Go, throw yourself into the sea,' and does not doubt in his heart but believes that what he says will happen, it will be done for him. Therefore I tell you, whatever you ask for in prayer, believe that you have received it, and it will be yours" (Mark 11:21-24).

"Faith that can move mountains" has become a cliché among Christians. However it is a phrase that can be misunderstood. What happens when we pray for mountains in our lives to be moved, and they are not? We sometimes tend to blame it on a lack of faith. "If only I could believe enough, then God would answer my prayers." This is not what Jesus teaches. This kind of attitude places the power in our faith or in our prayers, not in God.

Certainly Jesus warned against lack of faith when we pray. "Do not doubt in your heart," he says. But this must be understood in the context of all the biblical teaching on prayer. If God does not do what we ask in prayer, it may be because of our lack of faith. Or, it may be that we have asked for the wrong thing. Or, it may be that it is not God's will to give it to us. The point of this passage is not that prayer is a magical formula: asking + faith = mountains moved. The point is, prayer is talking with God, and we must always pray with his nature and will in mind.

Clearly, this passage urges us to have faith when we pray—to believe God will answer our prayer. Jesus' language here is exaggerated for effect (much like his "camel through the eye of a needle" language). I don't believe he wants us to move literal mountains, but he does want us to have faith in a God who can do what seems impossible. The mountains of depression, hopelessness, poverty, addiction, and pain may weigh on us more than all the Rockies combined. Yet God can move those mountains too. Jesus does not want us to pray only when we are at the end of our rope, but neither does he want us to stop praying even if the rope breaks. Nothing is too great for God. In prayer we must never doubt his power nor his goodness. No situation is too bleak for prayer. God moves mountains; prayer moves God.

God answers the prayer of faith, but sometimes that answer can only be seen through the eyes of faith. When we pray according to God's will, then we believe that even in those times when we cannot see the mountains of difficulty move, God has still given us his blessing.

Active Faith

In this time of fast food and instant replays, we're not used to waiting for things. Though God promises to answer our prayers, he doesn't guarantee delivery in thirty minutes. Jesus taught that our faith will be rewarded if we keep praying about important needs and concerns.

> Then he said to them, "Suppose one of you has a friend, and he goes to him at midnight and says, 'Friend, lend me three loaves of bread, because a friend of mine on a journey has come to me, and I have nothing to set before him.'
>
> "Then the one inside answers, 'Don't bother me. The door is already locked, and my children are with me in bed. I can't get up and give you anything.' I tell you, though he will not get up and give him the bread because he is his friend, yet

because of the man's boldness he will get up and give him as much as he needs.

"So I say to you: Ask and it will be given to you; seek and you will find; knock and the door will be opened to you. For everyone who asks receives; he who seeks finds; and to him who knocks, the door will be opened.

"Which of you fathers, if your son asks for a fish, will give him a snake instead? Or if he asks for an egg, will give him a scorpion? If you then, though you are evil, know how to give good gifts to your children, how much more will your Father in heaven give the Holy Spirit to those who ask him!" (Luke 11:5-13).

In this parable, Jesus contrasts God to a friend disturbed in bed at midnight. The friend will not give out of friendship, but he will give to get rid of the disturbing visitor. God is not like the sleepy, bothered friend. He wants to give us good things. We give our children good gifts, even though we are evil people. How much more will the good God, who is always available to us, give us good gifts!

---

*We are told to not give up,
perhaps for our own sake, to mold
our will to his.*

So the parable does not picture God as irritated or bothered by our prayers. The point of the parable is persistence. If being persistent pays off when dealing with ill, sleepy, evil men, then how much more will it pay off when we ask of our loving Father. God does not need to be told constantly of our needs to answer us. He knows them already. But we are told to not give up, perhaps for our own sake, to mold our will to his.

When people ask me why I believe in God, I tell a story of persistent prayer. From age fifteen to twenty, not a day went by without my praying to God to help me find a lifelong companion. I prayed for a woman who loved God and would love me, for one who would bring me closer to Jesus. At times, I thought I had found her but was disappointed. When I did meet her, I had no idea she was the one. It was two years before I even asked her out, then we dated for two years before we were married. Now I thank God every day for sending her to me and for blessing me with over seventeen years of marriage. I know she came to me as a gift from above, a gift I don't deserve. An answer to persistent prayer.

There is certainly a difference between persistence in prayer and the empty babbling Jesus warned of earlier. Jesus is not saying that fifty prayers are better than forty, as if God counts rather than listens to prayer. What he says is "don't stop praying," as is made clear in the next parable:

> Then Jesus told his disciples a parable to show them that they should always pray and not give up. He said: "In a certain town there was a judge who neither feared God nor cared about men. And there was a widow in that town who kept coming to him with the plea, 'Grant me justice against my adversary.'
>
> "For some time he refused. But finally he said to himself, 'Even though I don't fear God or care about men, yet because this widow keeps bothering me, I will see that she gets justice, so that she won't eventually wear me out with her coming!' "

And the Lord said, "Listen to what the unjust judge says. And will not God bring about justice for his chosen ones, who cry out to him day and night? Will he keep putting them off? I tell you, he will see that they get justice, and quickly. However, when the Son of Man comes, will he find faith on the earth?" (Luke 18:1-8).

Here Jesus contrasts God with an evil judge who cares nothing for others, but who will grant justice to a widow simply so she will leave him alone. If someone as rotten as this judge will vindicate the widow just because of her persistence, then how much more readily will the God of love grant justice to his chosen ones?

In Luke's day this parable would be good news indeed. Many in the early church had undergone ridicule, imprisonment, and torture for their faith. They had cried to God for justice, for vindication, but he had not yet rescued them. They were losing heart.

For us who live nearly 2000 years later, the parable is still welcome news. At times it seems that evil is triumphant in the world. As Christians, our lives are quite strange to those around us. People cannot understand why we do not live for the moment as they do. We forgo temporary pleasures—wealth, physical pleasures, power—because we believe a new world is coming. Yet it appears that the new world has been delayed; Christ has not yet returned, so we are tempted to lose heart. Those around us appear to have more fun, more life, indeed, even more sense than we do. They look like realists, and we look like dreamers, wishing for a world that does not exist. But we know better. We know the true reality, yet we long to be vindicated. We want those around us to see that our goals were

right all along. We want every knee to bow before
the Lord Jesus.

And so we can pray and not lose heart, for God
will speedily vindicate us. We pray in light of that
reality that unbelievers cannot see. We pray, knowing the Son of Man will return to grant justice. The
question is: will he find us faithful?

Humble Faith

If our answer to the above question is, Of course
he will find us faithful; if we feel our salvation is
assured because of our own righteousness or perhaps
even because of our "spiritual" prayers, Jesus warns
us in a third parable against spiritual pride in
prayer:

> To some who were confident of their own righ-
> teousness and looked down on everybody else,
> Jesus told this parable: "Two men went up to the
> temple to pray, one a Pharisee and the other a
> tax collector. The Pharisee stood up and prayed
> about himself: 'God, I thank you that I am not
> like other men—robbers, evildoers, adulterers—
> or even like this tax collector. I fast twice a week
> and give a tenth of all I get.'
>
> "But the tax collector stood at a distance. He
> would not even look up to heaven, but beat his
> breast and said, 'God, have mercy on me, a sin-
> ner.'
>
> "I tell you that this man, rather than the other,
> went home justified before God. For everyone who
> exalts himself will be humbled, and he who
> humbles himself will be exalted" (Luke 18:9-14).

Modern audiences are apt to hear this parable in
a way completely opposite to how it was heard

originally. To us the Pharisee is the bad guy from the beginning. When we hear *Pharisee*, we immediately think *hypocrite*. We don't expect his prayer to be answered. By contrast, we know that some tax collectors were companions to Jesus, so they can't be all bad.

Jesus' listeners would have known better. After all, the Pharisees were those who took God's word seriously. Their whole lives were spent in devotion to him. They kept the law in every detail. They gave to the poor. They fasted. Their motto was, "God said it; I believe it; that settles it." And they certainly knew how to pray.

Tax collectors were traitors. They took the hard-earned money from God's people and gave it to a pagan government. They did not care for God or his law, but lived only to line their own pockets. For a tax collector to pray would be a waste of time.

So this parable must have shocked those who first heard it, though it fails to shock us. It was unthinkable that a Pharisee's prayer would not be heard while a tax collector's would. But that is precisely what happened. "Everyone who exalts himself will be humbled, and he who humbles himself will be exalted."

Genuine prayer always involves true repentance. One of my students, Joel Petty, had been a missionary in Russia. He told the story once of a woman who came to him to be baptized. He asked her, "Do you repent of your sins?" She answered in Russian, "A little." When we pray, are we like the Pharisee who does not repent at all, like this woman who repents a little, or like the tax collector who really knew how to repent?

We modern Christians cannot really understand this parable unless we identify with the Pharisee.

Like him, we love God; we want to keep his law; we pray to him regularly. Like the Pharisee, we, too, are appalled by those who despise God's laws—rapists, child molesters, murderers, thieves, corrupt politicians—and we thank God we are not like them. We might even read this parable and thank God that we are not hypocritical like this Pharisee.

Only one is righteous.
It is the One to whom we pray.

But Jesus speaks this parable to us. Prayer must never be a time to rejoice in our own righteousness. Only one is righteous. It is the One to whom we pray. We come to this holy God in the filthy rags of our own righteousness. Yes, we are to approach him boldly. Yes, he is our loving Father. But we still always come with these words, "God, have mercy on me, a sinner!"

Jesus provides us with the courage and confidence to come to him, asking God in prayer for what we need. Following his teachings, we can grow in faith and come to understand how we are to pray. For Jesus promises that when we ask, he still teaches.

Focusing Your Faith:

1. What are some of the phrases you hear repeated often in prayer? What can you do to keep your prayer language fresh?

2. If someone other than God could have heard you pray yesterday, what would he or she think is really important to you?

3. Who are your enemies—national, local, and personal? How do you pray for them?

4. What has Jesus taught you about prayer today?

5. What stories of answered prayer in your own life have helped your "unbelief"?

6. What problem in your life seems insurmountable? Can't God move this mountain?

7. Ask the Lord to reveal any sin in your life. Confess the sin to him, and ask him to forgive you.

Chapter 3

Praying
with Jesus

The sign on the overworked tax accountant's cluttered desk read, "The hurrier I go, the behinder I get." And I thought of my own schedule and said a silent "Amen." It's true we live in a hurried society. Fami-

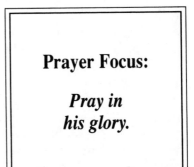

Prayer Focus:

*Pray in
his glory.*

lies are torn apart by work, sports, church functions, school, and a million other activities. While parents agree that it's important to spend time with their children, they can't seem to find the time. According to a recent Barna Research report, mothers spend an average of only fifty minutes per week in meaningful interaction with their teens. It's worse with fathers. Statistics show that fathers who live in the home with their teenage children spend only fifteen minutes per week in meaningful interaction. In single-parent homes the challenges are even more difficult. Few families actually sit down together for meals anymore. Fewer still are able to find time for private family devotionals or prayer. Instead, we set our prayer schedule on "crisis mode" and pray only when trouble hits.

We should be aware of the way our rushed Christian lives communicate to others. We don't want our neighbors to say, as author Jean Fleming's did, "We couldn't be Christians; we couldn't live at your pace."

Make Quiet Time

Christians today hear and talk quite a bit about "quiet time." We recognize the value of setting aside a time when we can be alone to pray to God and reflect on his Word without being interrupted. But few of us actually do it on a regular basis. It seems that our busy world of jobs, families, and pressures of modern life do not leave us the luxury of not being interrupted.

But no matter how busy we are, we cannot be busier than Jesus. Who among us is more popular than Jesus? Who has more demands on his time? Do we travel as much? Do we constantly have to deal with smothering crowds? Do we have no refuge, no "place to lay our head"?

Perhaps Jesus had a secret that we fail to grasp. We feel the need and even think it our right to go on vacation to get away from it all. Jesus never took a vacation. But he did make the effort to get away. He made time to pray. Oh, there's nothing wrong with a vacation, but sometimes we return from vacation exhausted, not invigorated. In our quest for time away, we might have overlooked the rejuvenating power that Jesus tapped into. If God is truly our Father, then we, like Jesus, must take time alone to talk with him. If we don't, we've missed the point of prayer and the essence of what being God's child is all about. We fail to find that true rest, relaxation, and rejuvenation that come from being on the mountain with God.

Jesus prayed public prayers, but he also had a habit of private prayer with God. After a day of healing the sick and feeding the five thousand, Jesus needed to get away from the crowd to be alone with his Father. "Immediately Jesus made the disciples get into the boat and go on ahead of him to the other side, while he dismissed the crowd. After he had dismissed them, he went up on a mountainside by himself to pray. When evening came, he was there alone" (Matthew 14:22, 23). Jesus practiced what he preached. He prayed not to be seen by others, but spoke to his Father privately.

Another time, after a long day of healing, Jesus rose early to be by himself to pray. "Very early in the morning, while it was still dark, Jesus got up, left the house and went off to a solitary place, where he prayed" (Mark 1:35). Jesus' popularity as a healer and teacher must have made it difficult for him to get away for prayer alone. "Yet the news about him spread all the more, so that crowds of people came to hear him and to be healed of their sicknesses. But Jesus often withdrew to lonely places and prayed" (Luke 5:15, 16).

Withdrawing to pray alone was a constant feature of Jesus' life. To him prayer was more than a religious ceremony to be done in the synagogue, more than a custom before meals or a ritual before bed, and certainly not a last resort in times of trial. Prayer was the lifeblood of Jesus. Whether late at night or early in the morning, Jesus felt drawn to be alone with his Father.

Isn't that what we really want, to be closer to God? Jesus made time to be with the Father because he longed to be with him. Jesus couldn't stand to be apart from God, apart from prayer. He knew those times of personal contact through prayer would give him peace and strength, no matter what the world threw at him. Too often we make time for God out of a sense of duty because we want or need something or because we're in trouble. Instead we should make time for prayer because we long with all our being to be close to our loving Father.

Give Thanks

In the Gospels, whenever Jesus distributes food, he first blesses it. At the feeding of the five thousand (Matthew 14:19) he "gave thanks and broke the loaves," and at the feeding of the four thousand (Matthew 15:36) "when he had given thanks, he broke them . . ." At the Last Supper, he "took bread, gave thanks and broke it, and gave it to his disciples, saying, 'Take and eat; this is my body' " (Matthew 26:26). Even the resurrected Jesus, when eating supper with the two disciples he met on the way to Emmaus, "took bread, blessed and broke it, and gave it to them" (Luke 24:30, NRSV).

It is easy to overlook the blessing of the food in these stories, because the stories themselves are so grand. In the first two stories, Jesus performs astounding miracles: He feeds five thousand and then four thousand people with a handful of food, but in each case he takes time to say the blessing. The Last Supper is poignant because it is the last time Jesus is with the disciples before his arrest and death. Jesus says the blessing for the bread and wine. But, more significantly, he begins a ritual repeated countless times in many places throughout the centuries—a ceremony known by many names, including the Eucharist, which means the "giving of thanks." In the Emmaus story, the blessing of the bread is so characteristic of Jesus that it opens the disciples' eyes to his true identity (Luke 24:31).

But what does it mean to "bless the bread"? In the New International Version passages, another term is used: to give thanks. When Jesus blessed bread, he gave thanks to the Father who provides. He not only teaches his disciples to pray for daily bread, but by his example teaches us to be grateful for it. Blessing the bread gives thanks to God and calls on him to bless it for his service. Our food comes from God and is also for God; we eat to live for him.

Prayer for food was once a habit among Christians. My family never ate a meal without "asking the blessing" first. Today, even for many Christians, this custom is fading away. Perhaps it is because we eat on the run so often; seldom do we have a sit-down meal with our families. But wasn't Jesus just as busy, as "on the run" as we are? Yet he took time to pray wherever he was.

Perhaps we neglect prayer for food because it seems so trivial, so trite, so rote. We pray the same prayer every time. After all, the first prayer most of us learned was, "God is great, God is good, let us thank him for our food." Such a prayer may seem childish to us now—so childish that we stop praying at mealtimes altogether. But wasn't prayer for food a habitual practice of Jesus? Yet did he not mean it every time?

Or perhaps we don't pray for food because we take it for granted. We've never been really hungry. Our refrigerators, pantries, and supermarkets are stocked. If we go six hours without eating, we say, "I'm starving." If we can't find our favorite snack

cakes in the pantry, we say, "There's nothing to eat."
Oh, some of us may have been through some hard
times, but we've probably never had to beg for food.
Jesus, who had the power to turn stones to bread,
still trusted the Father, not himself or others, to
provide. That's why he gave thanks for all he received. And when we begin trusting our Father to
provide, we will want to restore the habit of thanking God and asking his blessing on each meal we eat.

Ask for the Impossible

Jesus showed us that he prayed regularly for
daily needs and concerns, but he also prayed in
times of crisis. One of his most amazing miracle
stories is the raising of Lazarus from the dead. Jesus
hears Lazarus is ill, but waits two days until he
knows he is dead. He then takes his disciples to
Bethany where he meets Mary and Martha, the dead
man's sisters. He orders the stone removed from the
tomb, even though Lazarus has been dead four days.

> So they took away the stone. Then Jesus looked
> up and said, "Father, I thank you that you have
> heard me. I knew that you always hear me, but I
> said this for the benefit of the people standing
> here, that they may believe that you sent me."
>
> When he had said this, Jesus called in a loud
> voice, "Lazarus, come out!" The dead man came
> out, his hands and feet wrapped with strips of
> linen, and a cloth around his face.
>
> Jesus said to them, "Take off the grave clothes
> and let him go" (John 11:41-44).

So much is in this passage. Again we may overlook the prayer because of the greatness of the
miracle. And what a miracle! A man dead four days

is brought immediately back to life. But the miracle takes place only through prayer. It looks at first like Jesus is ignoring his own teaching about praying to be seen by others. After all, doesn't he say he is praying only for the benefit of the people? But no. He is not praying for publicity. What we have here is a public prayer that reflects a previous private prayer, a testimony that gives the glory to God.

Note closely what Jesus says: "Father, I thank you that you have heard me." Jesus had already prayed privately, asking the Father to raise Lazarus. He knew his Father had already answered that prayer. But he prays publicly, not so others might think him pious, but so they might know that the power of the miracle came from God and "that they may believe that you sent me."

> *Only those who call upon the*
> *invisible will see the impossible.*

This passage serves as a commentary on Jesus' own teaching on the power of prayer. No one, not the disciples, not the crowd, and certainly neither Mary nor Martha expected Lazarus to be raised. Even when Jesus plainly tells Martha, "Your brother will rise again," she misunderstands and thinks he is talking of the resurrection at the last day. No one can be raised from the dead. It is impossible! But Jesus did the impossible through prayer. Only those who call upon the invisible will see the impossible.

How many times do we fail to pray for the impossible? I have a boyhood friend. At one point we were closer than brothers, but our lives took different paths. I remember as a fifteen year old having long conversations with "Bob" (not his real name) about our mutual faith in Jesus and our excitement in studying the Bible (OK, I'll admit we were strange teenagers). But in later years he began to drink, alienated his family and friends, and became a complete recluse. I tried more than once to talk to him about his relationship to the Lord, but he always rebuffed me with laughter or with anger. Eventually, I confess, I gave up on Bob and even forgot about him in my prayers. He seemed beyond hope of change. Impossible.

As others continued to pray for Bob, an amazing thing happened. Like the demon-possessed man of old, the next time I saw him he was "in his right mind," having returned to the Lord and to the church.

Is there a Bob in your life? One who is as spiritually dead as Lazarus was physically dead? Don't stop believing in the power of prayer for him or her. The God who raised Lazarus by the power of Jesus' prayer can do what cannot be done.

Share in the Glory

We can hear Jesus' longest prayer in John 17. This beautiful prayer after the Last Supper and before his arrest, is, no doubt, typical of the way Jesus prayed privately to the Father. But this time he is in crisis. Having dismissed Judas the betrayer from the Supper, he plainly tells his disciples, "I will be with you only a little longer" (John 13:33). In John, this prayer is Jesus' final recorded prayer before the crucifixion. With the cross before him, he prays for himself and for all his disciples.

Glorify Jesus

In the first part of the prayer, Jesus recognizes

his work will soon be complete. As the ultimate High Priest, Jesus intercedes with God for himself. He looks toward heaven and prays:

> Father, the time has come. Glorify your Son, that your Son may glorify you. For you granted him authority over all people that he might give eternal life to all those you have given him. Now this is eternal life: that they may know you, the only true God, and Jesus Christ, whom you have sent. I have brought you glory on earth by completing the work you gave me to do. And now, Father, glorify me in your presence with the glory I had with you before the world began (John 17:1-5).

Jesus is so dedicated to going to the cross that he speaks as if the deed is already done: "I have brought you glory on earth by completing the work you gave me to do." He also displays his trust in God's faithfulness: since Jesus has completed his task, God will glorify him. This is an obvious reference to the resurrection. Although Jesus heads to the cross, he prays in faith that God's power will accomplish the impossible, that through this horrible death he will be brought to life and glory. As Christians take up the cross daily, we, too, in prayer must pray that Jesus be glorified and trust the faithful God who brings triumph and glory out of death and defeat.

Pray for Protection

Even facing death, Jesus thinks not of himself but of his disciples. The bulk of this prayer is for "those you have given me" (John 17:9). He had already promised these disciples that he would not leave them "orphaned," but would give them the Holy Spirit to teach and guide them (John 14:18-26).

Still he is concerned for the safety of the disciples, because he knows persecution awaits them:

> I have given them your word and the world has hated them, for they are not of the world any more than I am of the world. My prayer is not that you take them out of the world but that you protect them from the evil one. They are not of the world, even as I am not of it. Sanctify them by the truth; your word is truth. As you sent me into the world, I have sent them into the world. For them I sanctify myself, that they too may be truly sanctified (John 17:14-19).

Today we Christians do not always realize the precarious position we occupy in this world. Too many of us have made peace with this world and feel quite at home in it. In contrast to these "worldly Christians," the true disciple will always face danger from the world. Jesus foresaw this danger and prayed for God to protect his followers. We also should pray to God for strength and protection from a world that so easily distracts us from the business of discipleship.

Here is the essence of discipleship: God has sent us into the world, yet we do not belong in the world. God's Word, the Truth, has sanctified us—marked us off as God's own people—and the world hates us for it. But just as Christ loved the world and was sent into it, so we disciples are sent into the world for the sake of Christ.

Pray for Others

Jesus' words also teach us about intercessory prayer. Even when facing imminent death, Jesus thought of his disciples. How many of our own prayers, particularly during crises, are centered on others rather than on our own personal needs and wants? Like Jesus we must remember to pray for others. We must pray for their physical needs—for health and food. We must pray for their emotional needs—for peace and joy. We must pray, as Jesus did, for their spiritual needs, that God will keep them safe from the evil one. We must even pray for our enemies, for those still in the world, that their eyes may be opened to the love of God in Christ.

I was recently taught this lesson of concern for others by a boy at our church. Walt is a typical five year old, full of life and smart as a whip. Born with a bone weakness, last month he broke his leg for the fifth time. In a cast and in pain, Walt was told about an older woman in our church, a friend of his, who had passed away. "She'll have a new body!" he said with glee. Though his own body had betrayed him, Walt could rejoice with others. In the same way, facing death, Jesus thought of us.

Pray for Unity

If we could have heard Jesus praying, we would have heard him pray for unity—for the disciples of his day and also for us:

My prayer is not for them alone. I pray also for those who will believe in me through their message, that all of them may be one, Father, just as you are in me and I am in you. May they also be in us so that the world may believe that you have sent me. I have given them the glory that you gave me, that they may be one as we are one: I in them and you in me. May they be brought to complete unity to let the world know that you sent me and have loved them even as you have loved me.

> Father, I want those you have given me to be
> with me where I am, and to see my glory, the
> glory you have given me because you loved me
> before the creation of the world (John 17:20-24).

We who have believed in Christ through the
apostles' word are also included in this prayer. Jesus
prayed for us! Yet, in light of the current situation of
the church, his prayer is a challenge: he prays that
all believers may be one. Sadly, the history of the
church has mainly been one of disunity. Even today,
we spend much of our energy focusing on what
divides rather than what unites Christians. If Jesus
prayed for unity, then we cannot call him Lord and
at the same time fight with our Christian brothers
and sisters.

Christian unity begins with the unity of the
Father and the Son. Only by being in union with
them are we united with one another. And only in
that union will the world know the One whom God
sent (John 17:23). A wise Christian teacher once told
me that the problem with most Christians is that
they are too concerned with being "right." If I care
only that I am right and you are wrong, we can
never have unity. Instead, we can join Jesus in the
prayer for unity. We can ask God to change our
hearts as we focus on points of agreement rather
than disagreement.

Pray for Glory

But Christ prays an even more astonishing
prayer for us: he prays we will see him in his glory.
Jesus had faith that God would raise him from the
dead and would glorify him in heaven. This Jesus
who calls us to die with him also prays for us to
share in his resurrection and his glory.

Jesus concludes his prayer by speaking of love:

Righteous Father, though the world does not know you, I know you, and they know that you have sent me. I have made you known to them, and will continue to make you known in order that the love you have for me may be in them and that I myself may be in them (John 17:25, 26).

In the Lord's Prayer, Jesus prays that God's name will be made holy. Here he says he has made that holy name known to his disciples: that name is love. To know God is to know love. This is the essence of Jesus' prayer for us, that we love Jesus with the same love that the Father has for his Son. Jesus, the love of God incarnate, wants to be in us. What we, as a society, most need to do is to slow down and make time in our hurrier-I-go schedule to pray, and then bask in the soul-soothing glory of the Lord. He asks us to let him in. We pray God's love for Christ will fill our lives. We pray Christ will be in us.

*Jesus, the love of God
incarnate, wants to be in us.*

Jesus was a man of prayer—our perfect example. And we can know that when we pray, we are not only following Christ's example, we are also praying with him in his glory. And he is praying with us. We pray in his name. And, like him, we know our Father always hears us.

Focusing Your Faith:

1. How did mealtimes in your home growing up differ from mealtimes in your home today? How can you incorporate a touch of "the good old days" meals into your present diversified lifestyle?

2. What do you think is the best way to show God your thanks for food and life's necessities?

3. At the end of a busy week, what do you look forward to most for rejuvenating your tired body and soul?

4. How much time do you spend alone with God each day? Keep a record of your time spent in prayer this week.

5. When have you prayed for the impossible, and God granted your request? How did that change your prayer life?

6. What is your church doing in your community to encourage unity among believers? To glorify Jesus?

7. In your prayer journal, write down your most urgent prayer needs. Then write out your expectations of God.

Chapter 4

Jesus
Shows Me the Way

$\mathcal{T}$homas was introduced to gospel teachings at an early age. Through the influence of his itinerant-preacher father and his musically inclined mother and uncle, gospel music quickly became his first love.

Prayer Focus:

Pray in God's will.

But the more proficient he became in music, the more he was lured by money and fame. "I began to backslide," he later recalled, "and went on to Chicago, hoping to become a jazz musician. I worked at the theaters, wanting to be around the show folks where things were lively. During the first World War, I composed songs for blues singers and began to make money. I put a band together and . . . I wrote over 150 blues songs."

But he could not forget his Christian roots. One

night, following a police raid on a bar where he was working, he began to reevaluate his life. The turning point in his life came in 1921, when he recommitted his life to God and began writing gospel music.

In 1932 he had agreed to take part in a gospel meeting in St. Louis. On the day the meeting was to begin, he left home early in the morning, leaving his pregnant wife behind, expecting to see her again in a few days. He never saw her again. Instead, a telegram came saying his wife had died suddenly in childbirth, and the following night his newborn son died also.

His first reaction was to lash out at God. "I said, 'God, You aren't worth a dime to me right now.' " But soon he realized how much he needed the Lord, and it was in his grief that Thomas Dorsey wrote the lines to the favorite prayer song, "Precious Lord, Take My Hand." It was a song that comforted his own broken heart and reached out to others. "My business," he later wrote, "is to try to bring people to Christ instead of leaving them where they are. I write all my songs with a message."

We may think Jesus never had to struggle to find an answer to prayer, since he had a "direct pipeline" to God. We may think that his prayers are too "spiritual" to be an example for us at our turning points and in times of crisis. Jesus' prayers in Gethsemane prove otherwise. His are human prayers, the prayers of one who faithfully wrestles with the will of God. Jesus confided in his disciples, "My soul is overwhelmed with sorrow to the point of death. Stay here and keep watch with me" (Matthew 26:38).

Jesus came to show us how to live in communion with the Father. Now he is keeping watch with us, praying with us, as we struggle to pray and find answers.

Prayer at the Turning Points

Jesus spent regular quiet time with the Father, but as a human being he also knew times when prayer was a cry for special help and guidance. In the turning points of his life, in the crises, in those times of trial that determined what he was made of, Jesus prayed. It was precisely in those times of prayer and crises that Jesus was most fully revealed as the Son of God. It is not just coincidence that it is precisely in such times that our own discipleship is revealed.

Pledging Loyalty

The baptism of Jesus marked his entry into public life. It revealed him as "the one who is coming," the one for whom John the Baptist prepared the way. In baptism we see Jesus as a man, identifying with our sinful need for repentance. In baptism we see him as the beloved Son of God, pleasing to the Father.

The story of Jesus' baptism is a familiar one. What we may have forgotten about this familiar story is Luke's revelation that this all happened as Jesus was praying. "When all the people were being baptized, Jesus was baptized too. And as he was praying, heaven was opened and the Holy Spirit descended on him in bodily form like a dove. And a voice came from heaven: 'You are my Son, whom I love; with you I am well pleased' " (Luke 3:21, 22).

Prayer and baptism. How appropriate it is for Jesus to pray as he begins his public ministry. How appropriate for God to answer his prayer with the Spirit. (Jesus later said the Father would grant the Holy Spirit to those who asked; Luke 11:13). How appropriate for the Father to answer Jesus' prayer with a proclamation of his pleasure in the actions of his beloved Son.

Prayer and baptism. Not an odd combination for Jesus. And not an odd combination for his disciples. After all, isn't baptism itself a prayer, "an appeal to God for a good conscience, through the resurrection of Jesus Christ"? (1 Peter 3:21, NRSV). Baptism is our prayer for the greatest gift of all: our salvation. We pray that God by grace through the death of Jesus will now look upon us as his beloved children, and will pronounce himself "well pleased" with us. In baptism, Jesus pledged his will as one with the Father and began his public ministry with prayer for the help of the Spirit. In baptism, we, too, pledge our loyalty to God and receive the gift of the Spirit (Acts 2:38). Our baptism, like Jesus', is a prayer.

> **Baptism is our prayer for the greatest gift of all: our salvation.**

I was young when I was baptized, but the memories are forever etched in my heart. I remember every detail: putting on the baptismal clothes, the coolness of the water, and the smiles on my parents' faces. Most of all, I remember that feeling of spiritual cleansing, of knowing by his grace I was right with God. In our baptismal prayer and in each prayer afterward, we again can feel that assurance that God is now our Father. By grace, our past is gone. All things are new.

Making Decisions

Christians yearn to know God's will in times of decision. Does God want me to marry this person? Does he want me to take this job? To attend that congregation? To move to that city? To buy that house? The choice is made more difficult when other people are involved. When we must decide who should be promoted at work, who should lead our country, and who should lead our church, we need special wisdom and guidance.

Jesus, too, needed help from the Father at decision time. One of the most important decisions he made concerned those who would lead his flock after he departed. Whom should he choose to be apostles? No doubt, our choices would have been different. The ones he chose were something of a motley crowd: zealots, tax collectors, and fishermen. They were uneducated, rough, impulsive men. From a human point of view, none seemed suited for leadership.

But we know the rest of the story. We know that through the power of God and the gift of the Spirit, these leaders, these apostles, became champions of the faith and loving shepherds of the flock. They gave their lives to Jesus, their Lord and Master.

So how did Jesus make such a good decision? Did his insight into people make it easy? Was he just lucky? No. He made this decision through prayer: "One of those days Jesus went out to a mountainside to pray, and spent the night praying to God. When morning came, he called his disciples to him and chose twelve of them, whom he also designated apostles" (Luke 6:12, 13).

Since Jesus felt the need to spend all night in prayer to the Father before he made this momentous choice, we, too, need to seek the Father's will and guidance with our decision making. Too many times we make crucial decisions based only on earthly wisdom, on what seems best when we weigh our options. Or worse, we sometimes make choices based on an inward feeling—on how things strike us at the moment. Jesus shows us another way: pray about the decision and God will answer you. That answer may be consistent with conventional wisdom and our deepest feelings, or it may go counter to both.

> *Jesus shows us another way: pray about the decision and God will answer you.*

There is no simple formula for knowing how God helps in decision making. But Jesus believed in praying through the great decisions of his life. He trusted the Father. Thankfully we can too.

Knowing the Messiah

"Who is Jesus?" is the most important question in history. The way that we answer that question determines our destiny. In Jesus' own ministry, he revealed his identity gradually. Even the twelve he chose after prayer came to know Jesus' full identity only at the end of a slow process. The first full confession of the nature of Jesus came in response to a question he posed to the apostles during prayer:

> Once when Jesus was praying in private and his disciples were with him, he asked them, "Who do the crowds say I am?"
>
> They replied, "Some say John the Baptist; others say Elijah; and still others, that one of the prophets of long ago has come back to life."
>
> "But what about you?" he asked. "Who do you say I am?"
>
> Peter answered, "The Christ of God" (Luke 9:18-20).

This great confession of Peter is the foundation

for the church (Matthew 16:17, 18) and the foundation of our lives as Christians. To be a Christian is to
confess Jesus as the Christ, or Messiah, of God. Note
that this greatest of questions ("Who do you say I
am?") and the greatest of answers ("The Christ of
God") takes place when Jesus is praying. Through
prayer he reveals himself to the disciples. In prayer
we today also see Jesus as he truly is. Joining him in
prayer, we come to a deeper understanding of his
nature as our Savior from God.

Like Peter, we know who Jesus is. Or do we?
Peter had been a disciple of Jesus for quite a while,
but he still didn't fully understand the Lord. Many of
us have been Christians for years but our spiritual
lives have stagnated. We think we know Jesus
backward and forward, but do we really know him?
How can we see him as he really is? Through his
Word and through prayer. In prayer he is revealed
to our hearts as he was revealed to Peter.

I confess to being prone to night terrors. In the
still of the night, I toss and turn, beset by doubts
and fears. Is there a God? Does he care for me? What
happens after death? Does my life count for something? All these questions and more swirl through
my mind. I do believe, but I need reassurance. It
comes in prayer. Like Peter, I know Jesus is Lord
because he reveals himself to me when I pray.

Being Transformed

Soon after his confession of Jesus as Christ, Peter
(along with James and John) is allowed to see the
Messiah in all his glory:

> About eight days after Jesus said this, he took
> Peter, John and James with him and went up
> onto a mountain to pray. As he was praying, the

appearance of his face changed, and his clothes
became as bright as a flash of lightning. Two
men, Moses and Elijah, appeared in glorious
splendor, talking with Jesus. They spoke about
his departure, which he was about to bring to
fulfillment at Jerusalem (Luke 9:28-31).

Peter, again the spokesman, calls for memorial
dwellings to be built for Jesus, Moses, and Elijah. No
doubt Peter meant this to be a compliment to Jesus,
placing him on a par with the great lawgiver and the
great prophet. But Luke says Peter didn't know what
he was saying (Luke 9:33). To make things clear, just
like at Jesus' baptism, a voice speaks from a cloud
saying, "This is my Son, whom I have chosen; listen
to him" (Luke 9:35).

In prayer we not only see
Jesus, but God recognizes us as
he recognized his Son.

On the two great occasions where God announces
from heaven that Jesus is his Son, Jesus has been
praying. It is while Jesus is in prayer that God calls
him the Beloved. It is in prayer that he receives the
Spirit. It is in prayer that he is glorified. Luke is
telling us that believers have the same avenue to
God. In prayer we not only see Jesus, but God recognizes us as he recognized his Son. While praying, we,
too, are marked as children of God. Our clothes may
not glisten, and we may not meet any prophets, but
our hearts and minds are transfigured in prayer—
transfigured into the likeness of the Beloved Son to
reflect his glory.

Remembering the Faith

It was Passover and Jesus knew his time was near. He and his apostles met privately in an upstairs room to celebrate the Passover meal. As they reclined at the table eating, Jesus took the bread, gave thanks, and broke it, saying, "This is my body, given for you; do this in remembrance of me" (Luke 22:19). After the supper, he took the cup of wine, gave thanks, and offered it to them (Mark 14:23). With these prayers, Jesus instigated the Lord's Supper, a meal to serve as a reminder of his saving sacrifice and to provide a means of communion and unity within the body of Christ.

It is at this turning point that Jesus also announces that one of his own disciples—his friend—will betray him.

Even trusted Peter, who had earlier confessed Jesus as the Christ, would soon be denying him. Jesus confronts Peter, saying, "Simon, Simon, Satan has asked to sift you as wheat. But I have prayed for you, Simon, that your faith may not fail. And when you have turned back, strengthen your brothers" (Luke 22:31, 32).

Like Peter, when Satan asks Jesus for permission to test us, Jesus will pray for us that our faith will not fail. Our friends and family will forsake us, and we will forsake our Lord, but because he prays for us, we can always return. We may fail in our actions, but with Jesus' help our faith will not fail. And after we've been tested, our faith will be strengthened, and we can use what we've learned to strengthen others.

Struggling with God's Will

Jesus had faith in the Father's goodness. He

trusted God to bring him through death and to glorify him. But he also knew that prayer can change the mind of God.

Change God's mind? How can that be? Isn't God's mind unchangeable? He is perfect; how can he change his mind? I don't know. I do know that the Bible makes it clear that while God himself doesn't change, he does change his mind. God sends the prophet to tell Hezekiah he will die. Hezekiah turns his face to the wall, he cries and prays to God, and God grants him fifteen more years (2 Chronicles 32:24-26; Isaiah 38:1-6). God sends Jonah to warn the city of Nineveh of her destruction. The king and people of Nineveh repent in sackcloth and ashes, so "God changed his mind about the calamity that he said he would bring upon them; and he did not do it" (Jonah 3:10, NRSV).

---

*In prayer we affect
the mind of God.*

God can, has, and will change his mind. I believe this is the most profound biblical teaching on prayer —one that demonstrates clearly the amazing extent of God's love: in prayer we affect the mind of God. If not, why did Jesus pray his prayer in Gethsemane? If prayer does not affect God, why pray? Jesus served a God who is so powerful that he can even allow his mind to be changed by his children. Facing an unjust, shameful, and cruel death, Jesus prays to be delivered; he prays to change God's mind:

> Then Jesus went with his disciples to a place called Gethsemane, and he said to them, "Sit here while I go over there and pray." He took Peter

and the two sons of Zebedee along with him, and
he began to be sorrowful and troubled. Then he
said to them, "My soul is overwhelmed with
sorrow to the point of death. Stay here and keep
watch with me."

Going a little farther, he fell with his face to the
ground and prayed, "My Father, if it is possible,
may this cup be taken from me. Yet not as I will,
but as you will."

Then he returned to his disciples and found them
sleeping. "Could you men not keep watch with me
for one hour?" he asked Peter. "Watch and pray
so that you will not fall into temptation. The
spirit is willing, but the body is weak."

He went away a second time and prayed, "My
Father, if it is not possible for this cup to be taken
away unless I drink it, may your will be done."

When he came back, he again found them sleeping, because their eyes were heavy. So he left
them and went away once more and prayed the
third time, saying the same thing.

Then he returned to the disciples and said to
them, "Are you still sleeping and resting? Look,
the hour is near, and the Son of Man is betrayed
into the hands of sinners. Rise, let us go! Here
comes my betrayer!" (Matthew 26:36-46).

In Gethsemane Jesus struggles with the same
question that often confronts us: What is God's will
for us? We know God's ultimate will is for us to be
his sanctified people—his children—and live with
him in glory. But what is his will for us in time of
suffering? God loves us; surely he does not want us
to suffer. We are his children; he gives only good

gifts to us. However, the Bible makes it clear that pain and suffering can be for our own good. Yes, we are God's children, but "the Lord disciplines those he loves, and he punishes everyone he accepts as a son" (Hebrews 12:6). But surely not all suffering is God's will. How can we know whether it is or not? Can't God change his mind?

Jesus faced this same dilemma. He had predicted his own death and resurrection (Matthew 26:2, 32). He knew on one level that it was God's will for him to die on the cross. Yet he had to wonder, "Could God change his mind?" So, grieved and agitated, he prayed.

In this time of crisis and decision, Jesus had to face the Father, but he also wanted his disciples near. He particularly asks Peter, James, and John to share this burden of grief with him. All they could do was sleep. Many times before, Jesus had escaped from the disciples to be alone in prayer. This time he needed them to watch with him. But they would not. He was alone. Alone, but with his Father.

He prayed the first time, "If it is possible, may this cup be taken from me." There was still hope that the Father had changed his mind, that he had found another way, that it was possible for Jesus to avoid the cross. But if the Father wanted him to die, Jesus was willing.

After finding the disciples asleep, Jesus prayed a second time. This prayer is slightly different: "If it is not possible for this cup to be taken away unless I drink it, may your will be done." Jesus was coming to realize that there was no other way but through the cross. Through prayer, he was learning the will of the Father. He went and found the disciples asleep again; he prayed a third time; he saw the betrayer coming. Now he was ready for the crisis—

for the cross—because he had prayed for the will of his Father.

Jesus didn't change the mind of God; the Father still wanted him to bear the cross. Was Jesus' prayer a failure? Of course not. God heard his prayer, yet God did not change his mind. God did comfort and strengthen Jesus. He did not take the cup, but he did prepare the drinker. Our prayers may not always change the mind of God, that is why we pray like Jesus, "Your will be done." But God always hears our prayers and gives us what we need: sometimes relief, sometimes strength. Jesus found power in prayer, enough power to face the cross.

> *God always hears our prayers and gives us what we need: sometimes relief, sometimes strength.*

We Americans may never have to face this same situation. It is unlikely we will be called to die in obedience to God's will in our lifetime. But in other parts of the world Christians are being persecuted. And many early Christians faced their own Gethsemanes. The night before they were to be burned alive or thrown to lions or crucified like their Lord, they must have prayed this prayer, "Please let this pass, but your will be done." God willed that many believers be martyred, but through his grace in Christ he strengthened them to be faithful to death, just as he strengthened Jesus in the garden.

No, we may not be called upon to die, but in another way, we Christians today do face our own Gethsemanes. We may not suffer a horrible death for our faith, but we do face the battle of our will versus God's will. Our problem may not be knowing God's will, but doing it. Like Peter, we find our spirit willing, but our flesh weak. The cup we may want to pass is not persecution, but responsibility.

Such courage comes only through prayer. Like Peter, we have the best of intentions. Peter says, "Even if all fall away, I will not." Jesus tells him, "You yourself will disown me three times." Peter insisted emphatically, "Even if I have to die with you, I will never disown you" (Mark 14:29-31). We know the rest of the story. Peter does deny his Lord. He had the best of intentions; he was emphatic with his confession; he was with Jesus wholeheartedly. What kept him from faithfulness? He failed to pray. What did Jesus tell him in the garden? "Watch and pray."

Like Peter, we lack the courage of Jesus. We lack it because we fail to pray as Jesus prayed. We know God's will is for us to overcome temptation, to live for others, to do what is right. We know he calls us to be faithful to our spouses, to nurture our children, to care for the stranger, and to love the church. Unlike Christ, we agonize not over God's will, but over our own. But if he had the courage to go to a literal cross, then through him we can find the courage to take up the daily cross of obedience to the Father's will.

Bearing Your Cross

Prayer and the cross. They seem to go together. It is no surprise to find Jesus talking with his Father at the greatest crisis of his life. The first prayer from the cross is actually a cry: "About the ninth hour Jesus cried out in a loud voice, 'Eloi, Eloi, lama sabachthani?'—which means, 'My God, my God, why have you forsaken me?' " (Matthew 27:46).

This prayer is a cry of pain. The pain is so intense, the scene so memorable, that Matthew records the very words Jesus spoke in Aramaic, the household language of Jesus' disciples. In the past the Father had appeared in a cloud to proclaim Jesus as his "beloved Son." Now on the cross there is nothing but silence from the Father. At times we have all felt abandoned by God; we have all cried in pain. But Jesus was truly abandoned by God.

This prayer is a cry of love. It is Jesus' love for us that drives him to the cross. As Paul later says, "God made him who had no sin to be sin for us, so that in him we might become the righteousness of God" (2 Corinthians 5:21). Because our holy God loved us, he had to turn his back on his own Son, who was bearing not his own sins, but ours. What greater pain can there be than to be forsaken by God? What greater love can there be than to bear the pain for others?

This prayer is a cry of hope. Hope? Yes, for Jesus here is not using his own words but is quoting the first line of Psalm 22. Jesus knew his Scriptures, and we can be sure he quoted this verse with the entire psalm in mind. In Psalm 22, David cries to the Lord in pain, but (as in many of the psalms) this cry of pain ends in a confession of faith and hope in God. Though the psalmist feels forsaken, in truth he knows the Lord ". . . has not despised or disdained the suffering of the afflicted one; he has not hidden his face from him but has listened to his cry for help" (Psalm 22:24).

Jesus' cry sounds like a cry of hopelessness, but although he quotes only the first verse, he knows this psalm ends in hope. Despite being abandoned by his Father, Jesus knew that God heard his cry and would ultimately deliver him. And God did this by raising him from the dead.

In deep pain on the cross, even abandoned by his God, Jesus prayed a second prayer. This one was for the welfare of others, even those who crucified him: "Father, forgive them, for they do not know what they are doing" (Luke 23:34). He had taught, "Pray for those who persecute you." Here Jesus does exactly what he had preached. What greater example of forgiveness can there be?

If Jesus while on the cross can pray for the very people who condemned him, spat upon him, and drove the nails home, can we fail to pray for those who wrong us? Whom do you still hold a grudge against? Who is out to get you? Who belittles, ridicules, and ignores you? What are their names?

Pray for them.

Jesus' last prayer is exactly
what we would expect:
a prayer of trust in the Father's will.

Jesus' last prayer is exactly what we would expect: a prayer of trust in the Father's will. "Jesus called out with a loud voice, 'Father, into your hands I commit my spirit' " (Luke 23:46).

A few weeks ago I stood beside the hospital bed of a Christian sister facing brain surgery. I told her we were praying for her complete recovery and hoped she'd be back in church soon. She replied, "I appreciate that," then looking me in the eyes she calmly said, "but if things don't work out, I'm ready to go." Two weeks later she was dead.

I am awed and humbled by such faith, for I cannot say with my whole heart, "I'm ready to go."

But my prayer, our prayer, is that we have this sister's faith and the faith of Jesus: "Into your hands I commit my spirit." In other words, "I'm ready to go." Some day each of us will face death. May we face it this way, trusting the Father with our future.

Praying in the Name of Jesus

As we look to Jesus and follow his great example and teachings on prayer, we can't help but want to develop a Christlike prayer life and to trust God in prayer during our turning points and in our crises. And we hold a powerful key—we can pray in the name of Jesus (Matthew 18:19, 20; John 14:13, 14; 15:16; 16:23-27). What does that mean? "In Jesus' name" is not some magical phrase we use to end our prayers. To pray in his name means we pray with the power and authority of Jesus. When we pray, he prays with us. Our prayers are his, and his prayers ours.

We never pray alone. As we pray to our Father in heaven, Jesus and the Holy Spirit pray with us. When we pray to Jesus, we also pray with the Spirit to the Father. If we ever feel alone in prayer, we must remember the one who constantly teaches us to pray.

As we turn to the rest of the New Testament to look at the prayers of the early church, let us remember that these, too, are the prayers of Jesus. When the disciples prayed, he prayed with them. As we learn to pray from them, we also are learning to pray like him.

Focusing Your Faith:

1. Why is it necessary to pray that God's will be done if he says, "Ask and it will be given"?

2. The last time your prayer was not answered the way you asked, what did God do for you instead?

3. How has Jesus revealed himself to you in prayer recently?

4. When have you been tested by Satan and failed? How did the Lord bring you back? Who did you help after your return?

5. What has been the greatest turning point in your life? How were you changed by it?

6. What decision are you struggling with today? If God opened a door for you right now, would you be ready to go through it?

7. Prayer is warfare. Aim your prayer at each of your problems and ask God to defeat them.

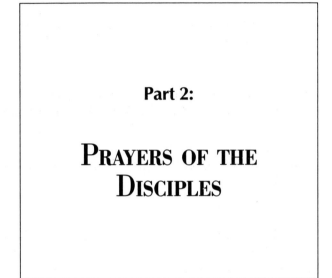

Part 2:

Prayers of the Disciples

Chapter 5

Leap

into the Fire

$\mathcal{W}$hen the emperor decreed that everyone must worship pagan gods, Apollonia refused. She was imprisoned and tortured mercilessly. The officials beat her jaws, breaking out all her teeth. When she still

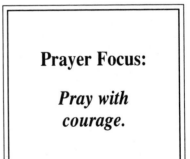

Prayer Focus:

Pray with courage.

refused to give in, they built a fire, threatening to burn her alive unless she would repeat their pagan expressions. But she never faltered. Instead, she chose to leap boldly into the fire rather than to betray her Lord.

Many early Christians faced death as they boldly professed their faith. Eusebius, church historian, recorded the life of this martyr in Alexandria, a city in North Africa. What power these early Christians had! What courage! What was their secret? Loyalty to Jesus? Of course. The power of the Spirit? Certainly. But they also knew the secret of prayer. The early church was a praying church. That was the source of their power. If we are to recapture their faith and their witness, we must learn to be constant in prayer.

Witnessing Jesus

Acts is the story of the church. The story of the church is the story of prayer. When we study it, we generally concentrate on the conversion stories or on Paul's missionary journeys. But Acts is a much richer book, containing a wealth of insight on what it means to be a community of disciples, and what it means to pray.

We need to mine that wealth. To do so, we must keep two facts about Acts in mind. First, the theme of Acts is being witnesses for Jesus. At the beginning of the book, Jesus appears to the apostles for the last time saying, "You will receive power when the Holy Spirit comes on you; and you will be my witnesses in Jerusalem, and in all Judea and Samaria, and to the ends of the earth" (Acts 1:8).

This apostolic witness through the power of the Spirit is carried on in spite of fierce opposition. Not only the apostles, but other disciples also "preached the word wherever they went" (Acts 8:4). No threat could stop their witness, for their courage came not from themselves but from the Father, Son, and Spirit through prayer.

The second important fact to remember about Acts is that it is the second volume in a two-volume work. Luke tells the story of Jesus in his Gospel and the story of the church in Acts. But the two stories are one. Acts is really a fifth Gospel, displaying

Jesus' actions on earth after his ascension. It is Jesus who sends the miracles and the Spirit at Pentecost. Jesus' name is called at baptisms and at healings. He did not end his work at Calvary, or at the empty tomb, or even at his ascension. Yes, Jesus is coming again, but in a sense he never left: he lives in the world through the church.

> *As the disciples witness for Jesus, they become one with him. His ministry becomes their ministry—his prayers, their prayers; his courage, their courage.*

As we watch the church pray in Acts, we watch Jesus pray as well. Luke goes to great pains to demonstrate that the church does what Jesus did. As the disciples witness for Jesus, they become one with him. His ministry becomes their ministry—his prayers, their prayers; his courage, their courage.

Praying with Courage

Since the church is to pray like Jesus prayed, we are not surprised to find them constantly at prayer. In Acts, the disciples have the same devotion to prayer that Jesus had modeled. "They all joined together constantly in prayer, along with the women and Mary the mother of Jesus, and with his brothers" (Acts 1:14). In Acts 1, the disciples are a confused lot, still expecting Jesus to set up an earthly kingdom (Acts 1:6). At the ascension, we find them gawking toward heaven, unsure of what to do (Acts 1:10). They are a small group, about 120 persons, not much on which to build a worldwide movement. They had not yet received the power of the Spirit. But in spite of their limitations, these disciples had courage, and they had learned at least one thing from the Master —they needed constantly to pray.

> *They approached God with courage*
> *because they trusted him.*

This prayer practice continues after Pentecost and spreads to the new disciples: "They devoted themselves to the apostles' teaching and to the fellowship, to the breaking of bread and to prayer" (Acts 2:42). The converts at Pentecost were all Jews; they knew their Jewish prayers, but they needed to learn to pray as Jesus prayed. Many of these converts knew little of what Jesus had taught the apostles. Imagine their shock in learning they must pray for their enemies. Imagine their excitement at hearing the Lord's Prayer for the first time. Imagine Peter, James, and John telling of the prayer, the glory, the visitors, and the voice at the Transfiguration. Through the apostles, these converts learned to pray by following Jesus' example. And they, like the apostles, learned to devote themselves to prayer.

The apostles were effective because they were more than teachers of prayer. They approached God with courage because they trusted him. When a dispute arose in the church concerning distribution of food to widows, seven men were appointed to take care of this problem so the apostles could "devote [themselves] to prayer and to serving the word" (Acts 6:4, NRSV). Caring for the poor is certainly an act close to the heart of God, but so is prayer. The early church neglected neither.

Like Christ, the early Christians were constant in

their daily walk with God. So when they needed God's special blessing and guidance for their tough decisions, challenges, and even persecution, they knew exactly where to turn. Let's examine some of those times.

Selecting Leaders

The church today needs guidance when selecting leaders. We tend to choose leaders for the church on the basis of their leadership in the wider community. If they are successful business leaders, we assume they will be good church leaders. In most churches, the congregation has a loud voice in selecting leaders. There is no politics like church politics. The process sometimes even degenerates into a democratic one—the candidate who gets the most votes wins.

*The church is not the world,
and church leaders are to have a different
authority from worldly leaders.*

But the church is not the world, and church leaders are to have a different authority from worldly leaders. The early church in Acts knew the loudest voice in choosing leaders must not belong to the congregation, but to Christ. They sought his voice in prayer.

Even before Pentecost, the 120 disciples had an important decision to make: who should take Judas's place as apostle. This decision was a crucial one. The full number of the apostles had to be complete to set the stage for Pentecost. To be one of the apostles was an awesome responsibility; they were to be witnesses for Jesus throughout the world.

They proposed candidates based on certain quali-
fications, but the final decision they left to Jesus:

> So they proposed two men: Joseph called Bar-
> sabbas (also known as Justus) and Matthias.
> Then they prayed, "Lord, you know everyone's
> heart. Show us which of these two you have
> chosen to take over this apostolic ministry, which
> Judas left to go where he belongs." Then they cast
> lots, and the lot fell to Matthias; so he was added
> to the eleven apostles (Acts 1:23-26).

Just as Jesus had chosen the original Twelve, it
is Jesus who picks Matthias. The disciples were not
qualified to make this choice; Jesus alone knows the
heart. So they pray and cast lots. The lot falls on
Matthias. He is numbered with the Twelve.

What exactly are lots? They were probably stones
of different color, shape, or marking. These stones
were placed in a receptacle, probably a bag, and then
the bag was shaken until a lot was thrown (cast) out.
In this case, there were two stones, a Joseph lot and
a Matthias lot, in the bag. Matthias's lot was thrown.

Why don't Christians cast lots today? I'm not
sure. Perhaps we associate it with chance, supersti-
tion, or magic. The Bible never makes these associa-
tions when the lot is cast in prayer. To cast lots is to
leave the decision to the Lord: "The lot is cast into
the lap, but its every decision is from the LORD"
(Proverbs 16:33). This may be the real reason we are
reluctant to cast lots today: we trust our own judg-
ment more than we trust the Lord's.

However, there may be a good reason for not
casting lots. The choosing of Matthias is the last
time this practice is mentioned in the Bible. On
Pentecost, the Holy Spirit comes upon the apostles
and is promised to all who repent and are baptized

(Acts 2:38). In the rest of Acts, leaders are chosen not by prayer and lots, but by prayer and the Spirit. In Acts 6, the church chooses leaders "full of the Spirit," and these seven men are appointed by the apostles through prayer and the laying on of hands (Acts 6:1-6).

Later, in Antioch, during prayer and worship the Spirit chooses Barnabas and Saul for a special work. They also are sent out on their mission with prayer, fasting, and the laying on of hands (Acts 13:1-3). On their mission, Paul and Barnabas in turn appoint elders in each church "with prayer and fasting" (Acts 14:23).

In fasting and prayer, we come to know the Father's will.

We can learn from these early Christians that our churches need strong leaders, strong servants who will give their lives in witness for Jesus. Choosing good leaders is one of the most important things a church can do. Our choices shouldn't be based on earthly standards but on the will of God. We can know his will through Scripture and through prayer. If Jesus prayed all night before selecting the apostles, if the Jerusalem church prayed as it cast lots for Matthias, if the early Christians prayed when choosing and appointing leaders, then we also must pray that the decision concerning Christian leaders will be the Lord's alone.

Although these passages primarily focus on prayer in selecting leaders, two practices associated with prayer are mentioned in passing. One practice is fasting. While fasting is seldom observed today, examples of it are sprinkled throughout both Testaments. Here in Acts, however, we note only that fasting is closely related to prayer. Fasting does much for the body and the soul. One important thing it does is to clear our minds so we can concentrate on the source not only of our food but of our life—God. In fasting and prayer, we come to know the Father's will.

The other practice associated with prayer is the laying on of hands. At first, this custom seems to signify that some power inherent in the apostles is passed on to another. However, laying on of hands is always accompanied by prayer. No human has power in himself to appoint someone to a position of leadership in the church. Laying on of hands with prayer signifies that the appointment is made not by men, but by God alone. He chooses leaders. He appoints leaders. Their power does not come from human authority, but from God and Christ, through the Spirit.

Suffering Persecution

The Christians in Acts faced great persecution. They lived from moment to moment knowing they might be called on to suffer and even to die for their witness for Jesus. The word *martyr* itself comes from the Greek word "witness." In their moments of pain, it was prayer that sustained these early disciples.

Praying for Boldness

The first mention of opposition to Christians is in Acts 4 where Peter and John are arrested for healing a lame man in the name of the resurrected Jesus. The Jewish authorities order them not to preach in the name of Jesus. They reply, "We cannot help speaking about what we have seen and heard" (Acts

4:20). Astounded by their boldness, the authorities threaten and release them.

After their release, Peter and John find the other disciples, recount their story, and pray together:

> Now, Lord, consider their threats and enable your servants to speak your word with great boldness. Stretch out your hand to heal and perform miraculous signs and wonders through the name of your holy servant Jesus.

> After they prayed, the place where they were meeting was shaken. And they were all filled with the Holy Spirit and spoke the word of God boldly (Acts 4:29-31).

What would our prayer be in a similar situation? If imprisoned and commanded to speak no more of Jesus, would we pray for safety? Would we ask God to change the hearts of the officials? Would we ask for persecution to cease? The disciples ask for none of these. They pray for one thing: for boldness to speak God's word. They pray not for an easier path, but for the courage and power to walk the path Jesus walked.

They pray not for an easier path,
but for the courage and power
to walk the path Jesus walked.

And they are answered! The house shakes, the Spirit fills them, and they do speak with boldness. Today's church needs to be shaken. Today's church needs boldness. We face little persecution for our faith, yet our Christian witness is often tentative and apologetic. We believe in Christ, but we don't want to "force that belief on others." Many Christians have bought into our culture's teaching that one faith is as good as another. We have abandoned, or at least apologized for, the exclusiveness of Christianity: that no other name but Jesus can save. We need courage to speak what we have seen and heard, to proclaim the good news of Jesus. We need the courage that comes only through prayer.

I've never really been persecuted for the faith, but I've seen persecution in the face of a teenage girl in a country that no longer exists. A few years ago I visited a small house church in East Germany. The church worshiped quietly, in fear of the secret police. The family in whose house they met had a beautiful and bright sixteen-year-old daughter. She was at the top of her class in school, but she would not be allowed to go to college because as a Christian she refused to join the Communist Party.

You might expect Christians in such a situation to be discouraged and downtrodden. No way! Those Christians' worship was the most joyous I have ever seen. And they knew how to pray. Although I didn't understand most of what they said, the reverence, sincerity, and unabashed joy of their prayers will stay with me forever. They knew the courage that comes through prayer.

Praying for Deliverance

Our heavenly Father not only grants courage in persecution, he also can deliver us from evil. In Acts 12, King Herod throws Peter in prison, intending to have him executed. Many disciples meet at the house of Mary, the mother of John Mark, to pray for Peter's release. God hears their prayer and sends an angel to free Peter. Peter then comes to Mary's house:

Peter knocked at the outer entrance, and a servant girl named Rhoda came to answer the door. When she recognized Peter's voice, she was so overjoyed she ran back without opening it and exclaimed, "Peter is at the door!"

"You're out of your mind," they told her. When she kept insisting that it was so, they said, "It must be his angel."

But Peter kept on knocking, and when they opened the door and saw him, they were astonished. Peter motioned with his hand for them to be quiet and described how the Lord had brought him out of prison (Acts 12:13-17).

The disciples' lack of faith is almost humorous. They are praying for Peter's release, but they don't believe it when he actually comes to their door. But they still had enough faith to pray, and God answered them more quickly than they could imagine. Isn't it ironic that this occurred during the Passover Feast, when the Jews were celebrating God's power to liberate! And yet these Jewish Christians were still shocked and amazed!

This story illustrates the power of God and the power of prayer. God grants courage to those who are persecuted, but if he wills, he can remove the persecution. It is always right to pray "deliver us from evil," if we also pray "your will, not ours, be done." God miraculously delivers Peter and later delivers Paul and Silas from prison while they are "praying and singing hymns to God" (Acts 16:25-34). Prayer can do what seems impossible. At times we may be like the disciples at Mary's house, praying when the situation seems hopeless. But we must not stop praying.

Praying with Your Last Breath

Yet God does not always set the prisoners free. He sometimes wills his followers to give the last full measure of their devotion. These martyrs, these witnesses for Jesus, find strength and comfort in prayer, even at the point of death, just as Jesus himself prayed on the cross. While being stoned to death, Stephen echoes the prayer of Jesus on the cross: "While they were stoning him, Stephen prayed, 'Lord Jesus, receive my spirit.' Then he fell on his knees and cried out, 'Lord, do not hold this sin against them.' When he had said this, he fell asleep" (Acts 7:59, 60).

Notice that he not only prays the prayer of Jesus from the cross, but he also prays to Jesus. We pray to God our Father, but we also, like Stephen, pray to Jesus. He intercedes for us, taking our prayers to our Father. We should follow Stephen's example and pray like Jesus, pray with Jesus, and pray to Jesus.

The early church was a suffering church. They considered it a joy to suffer for Jesus. They prayed for boldness to witness, no matter what the cost. Some even gave their lives for Jesus, praying to him with their last breath. Ignatius was thrown to the lions. Polycarp, an eighty-six-year-old saint, respected even by his persecutors, was burned at the stake. Perpetua, a noblewoman, and Felicitas, a slave, were martyred together at Carthage. Old and young, rich and poor, these early Christians gave their full devotion to God.

The modern church, at least in America, is a satisfied church. Fat and happy, we cannot imagine the possibility of martyrdom. The greatest persecution most of us face today is embarrassed looks, caustic comments, and perhaps a cold shoulder or two. But these puny trials are often enough to keep us quiet about our faith. When fear of failure, rejection, or not having the right answers keeps us from being bold, prayer gives us the courage to rely on Jesus for help. Perhaps, like Apollonia, instead of waiting for the fire of persecution to come to us, we should choose to leap boldly into the fire of our own accord. We may never face being a martyr, but that should not keep us from praying for a martyr's courage!

Only through prayer can we capture the boldness of these early Christians. Only through prayer can we share their trust in a Father who delivers us from all opposition, even from death itself.

Praying with Your Church Family

Group prayer is a particular blessing from God. Something special happens when Christians pray together—we become closer to God and to one another. Having left Ephesus after spending two years there, Paul returns to Miletus on his way to Jerusalem. From there he sends for the elders of the Ephesian church, seeing them for what he thinks will be the last time:

> When he had said this, he knelt down with all of them and prayed. They all wept as they embraced him and kissed him. What grieved them most was his statement that they would never see his face again. Then they accompanied him to the ship (Acts 20:36-38).

What a heartrending prayer this must have been. Just a few days later, Paul is to repeat this scene with the Christians at Tyre (Acts 21:5, 6). Like Paul, we know the church is a family. But what makes us family is a common Father. When we all pray, we are united with our Father and with each other. No doubt Paul and the Ephesians prayed that God would protect them. No doubt they prayed to be reunited in heaven—their true home. But they were one in prayer. Nothing can really separate us from our Christian brothers and sisters. No matter how far away from us they may be—in this world or the next—we are one with them in prayer.

Most modern churches have an abundance of ministries: worship ministries, education ministries, youth ministries, older-adult ministries, family life ministries, ministries to the poor, the homeless, and the sick. What about a ministry of prayer? Imagine what would happen if certain people in the church were designated "prayer ministers" who, like the apostles, would devote themselves to prayer. People who are troubled could call and ask them to pray with and for them. These "prayer ministers" would also diligently pray for the various ministries of the church, as well as its special challenges. The church would be electrified!

Focusing Your Faith:

1. How bold do you think Christians should be in local politics? School politics? National politics?

2. What do you think people in your church would say if the decision were made to choose the next minister by the casting of lots?

3. If you were to tell a new Christian what to expect in the Christian life, what would you say?

4. When you feel like giving up, what keeps you going?

5. How has your church "suffered for Christ"? Have you noticed any changes because of it?

6. How have you personally "suffered for Christ"? How has it matured you?

7. What can you as an individual do for those Christians in the world who are really suffering for Christ? As a family? As a church?

Chapter 6

Listen

to the Saints

I have an aunt who's known for giving bad presents (if she's reading this, I hope she doesn't recognize herself). As a kid at Christmas, I knew she'd give me clothes, not toys. Adults should know that kids want toys at

Prayer Focus:

Pray with the Spirit.

Christmas! As a teenager, she continued to give me clothes, things I wouldn't be caught dead in. As an adult, I could fill a small museum with the strange gifts she's given: fish ties, Elvis plaques, cuff links (who wears those anymore?), pet rocks, you name it. I could fill a museum—if I'd kept her gifts. I didn't. Fortunately, she lives far enough away that I don't have to explain the absence of her gifts from my house. Of course, I never told her that her gifts were junk; I just smiled and said thank you like my mama taught me.

Fortunately, God is not at all like my well-meaning but misguided aunt. God gives good gifts. All his gifts are good, but one is best. Jesus promises that the Father will give the greatest gift, the Holy Spirit, to those who ask. "If you then, though you are evil, know how to give good gifts to your children, how much more will your Father in heaven give the Holy Spirit to those who ask him!" (Luke 11:13).

The Gift of the Holy Spirit

Prayer and the Holy Spirit are connected throughout the New Testament. At Jesus' baptism, the Spirit descends on him while he is praying. Through prayer, the Spirit works in selecting church leaders. Later, in the epistles, we find that the Spirit helps us when we pray, interceding with God for us. We are not surprised to find that Jesus' promise that God will send his Spirit is fulfilled in prayer:

> When the apostles in Jerusalem heard that Samaria had accepted the word of God, they sent Peter and John to them. When they arrived, they prayed for them that they might receive the Holy Spirit, because the Holy Spirit had not yet come upon any of them; they had simply been baptized into the name of the Lord Jesus. Then Peter and John placed their hands on them, and they received the Holy Spirit (Acts 8:14-17).

The power to give the Holy Spirit was not in the apostles but in God. Only after Peter and John prayed for them did the Samaritans receive the Spirit. We, too, must take Jesus at his word and pray that the Holy Spirit will live in us, guide us, and empower us. This is God's greatest gift because it is the Spirit who makes us children of God.

Pray for Forgiveness

Not everyone understood about the giving of the
Spirit. While there is some mystery to the coming of
the Spirit (like the wind, it "blows wherever it
pleases," John 3:8), one man completely misunderstood the process. His name was Simon, and, being a
magician, he thought the Spirit came magically
through Peter and John. Simon must not have
grasped the role of prayer in the giving of the Spirit;
it came from God, not man. He offered money to
Peter and John to buy this "magical" power:

> Peter answered: "May your money perish with
> you, because you thought you could buy the gift of
> God with money! You have no part or share in this
> ministry, because your heart is not right before
> God. Repent of this wickedness and pray to the
> Lord. Perhaps he will forgive you for having such
> a thought in your heart. For I see that you are full
> of bitterness and captive to sin."

> Then Simon answered, "Pray to the Lord for me so
> that nothing you have said may happen to me"
> (Acts 8:20-24).

He may not have understood the role of prayer in
giving the Spirit, but Simon did understand Peter's
response and his call to repentance. Peter tells Simon
to pray for forgiveness. Simon must have felt unworthy to do so; he asks Peter to pray to the Lord for him.

Saul is another who prays for forgiveness. He had
committed the worst sin imaginable. He had blas-
phemed Jesus and murdered his followers. On the
way to Damascus to capture more Christians, Saul is
suddenly struck blind by a bright light and hears a

voice from heaven, a voice that identifies itself as "Jesus, whom you are persecuting." He is told to go into the city and wait for instructions (Acts 9:1-9).

For three days Saul does not eat or drink. We are told "he is praying" (Acts 9:11). We are not told what he prayed, but surely one thing was uppermost in his mind: the need for forgiveness. Saul had thought Jesus was a fake, a false Messiah who led people astray. Out of a mistaken zeal for God, he had imprisoned and killed those who spoke of Jesus' resurrection. Now he had heard the voice of the resurrected Christ. Now he knew himself not as a faithful crusader for God's truth, but as a murderer of the faithful, an enemy of the true Messiah sent by God. All that Saul had fought for was a lie. His life was turned upside down. No wonder he fasted and prayed.

How could God hear the prayers of such a sinner? But God heard and answered. Ananias came. Saul received his sight. He was baptized, "calling on his name," (Acts 22:16) and was filled with the Holy Spirit (9:17).

> *Since God hears the pleas of sinners like Simon and Saul, surely then he hears our pitiful cries for mercy.*

Since God hears the pleas of sinners like Simon and Saul, surely then he hears our pitiful cries for mercy. Saul, later known as Paul, calls himself the chief of sinners—not to compare himself to his peers or even to us today, but to offer us an invitation to inspect our own lives and confess our own desperate need for God's healing forgiveness. Like Simon and

Saul, we pray the tax collector's prayer, "Lord, be merciful to me, a sinner." And like the tax collector, we go away justified, forgiven by our gracious God.

Pray for Healing

"It's a miracle!"

Such a phrase scares many of us today. We may have seen too many fake miracle workers. Although we are Christians, we may think that God worked miraculously only in the past and now works only through "natural law." But the same God who worked in Jesus through prayer also worked in the apostles. He's the same God who works his mighty power in us today.

Jesus had promised power to the apostles, power through the Spirit that enabled them to do "many wonders and miraculous signs" (Acts 2:43). In the Gospels, these same apostles had trusted their own power and so were unable to heal the boy with a demon (Mark 9:18). In Acts, they have learned the lesson Jesus taught them, "This kind can come out only by prayer" (Mark 9:29). Through the power of God, the apostles perform the same miracles Jesus performed. They can even raise the dead! When a loving disciple named Tabitha (or Dorcas in Greek) dies, the church calls for Peter, who raises her from the dead. But like Jesus at Lazarus's tomb, he does so only through prayer:

> Peter sent them all out of the room; then he got down on his knees and prayed. Turning toward the dead woman, he said, "Tabitha, get up." She opened her eyes, and seeing Peter she sat up. He took her by the hand and helped her to her feet. Then he called the believers and the widows and presented her to them alive. This became known

all over Joppa, and many people believed in the Lord (Acts 9:40-42).

Tabitha is raised from the dead. As with Lazarus, her resurrection leads many to believe.

Other healings took place through prayer. Paul, like Peter, performs miracles similar to those of Jesus: "It so happened that the father of Publius lay sick in bed with fever and dysentery. Paul visited him and cured him by praying and putting his hands on him. After this happened, the rest of the people on the island who had diseases also came and were cured" (Acts 28:8, 9, NRSV).

It's clear in Acts that healing took place in prayer. Today we may have no one with the power of a Peter or a Paul, but we still pray for healing, and we still have the power that was in Peter and Paul: the power of Jesus through the Holy Spirit. Sometimes, particularly when doctors pronounce a case hopeless, Christians are reluctant to pray for healing. But we must not doubt the power and goodness of God. When all is hopeless, God can heal. And he will heal, through prayer.

We can experience a comfort and peace even in trial when we allow him to answer our prayers according to his will.

However, prayer is much more than a last resort. If we pray only when things are hopeless, we miss the point of prayer. And prayer is more than mere magic. God is powerful; he can heal. God is good; he wants to heal. But God is also God. He alone is the sovereign ruler of the universe. We pray that his will, not ours, will guide us.

Tabitha is raised from the dead. Stephen is not. Publius's father is instantly healed of sickness. Paul (who healed him) is himself not relieved of his own "thorn in the flesh." Peter is released from prison. James remains in prison and is beheaded. Acts is not the story of a constantly triumphant church. Prayer is not a sure formula for health, wealth, and success. Yes, we should pray in faith for healing, but we must pray for our will to be brought into alignment with God's will.

When we are healed, it is by his power. When we are not, it is still his power through prayer that sustains us. Even when we have no outward signs of healing or relief, he changes the way we view our suffering. He transforms us and our thinking to see an even greater blessing. We can experience a comfort and peace even in trial when we allow him to answer our prayers according to his will.

Luke carefully makes the point in Acts that healing power comes from Jesus, not from the apostles themselves. Today, some who claim to heal forget the power is God's. Though there may be many "fake healers" we must not let our cynicism keep us from praying to the true source of health: our Father in heaven.

Pray for Guidance

Does God hear the prayer of a sinner? I certainly hope so! All of us are sinners. Certainly God hears and forgives us when we pray. But does God hear the prayer of one who is not a Christian? If that person has finally rejected Christ, certainly not. If one rejects Jesus, how can one pray in his name? But what about the person who wants to do right, to follow Jesus, but does not know how?

Ah, that's different. There are many in our world

who have some idea of God, but do not know Jesus.
What should such a person do?

There is such a person in Acts; his name is
Cornelius. What he does is pray for guidance:

> At Caesarea there was a man named Cornelius, a
> centurion in what was known as the Italian
> Regiment. He and all his family were devout and
> God-fearing; he gave generously to those in need
> and prayed to God regularly. One day at about
> three in the afternoon he had a vision. He dis-
> tinctly saw an angel of God, who came to him and
> said, "Cornelius!"
>
> Cornelius stared at him in fear. "What is it,
> Lord?" he asked.
>
> The angel answered, "Your prayers and gifts to
> the poor have come up as a memorial offering
> before God. Now send men to Joppa to bring back
> a man named Simon who is called Peter. He is
> staying with Simon the tanner, whose house is by
> the sea" (Acts 10:1-6).

God definitely hears Cornelius's prayers (Acts
10:30, 31). Cornelius sends for Peter whom God has
prepared through a vision (Acts 10:9-16). When
Peter arrives, he preaches the gospel to Cornelius
and his family. The Spirit falls upon them, and they
are baptized (Acts 10:34-48). God hears the prayers
of everyone who seeks him. If we do not know how to
walk with God, we simply pray for guidance. God
might not send a Peter, but in some way he will
show us how to serve him. This is true not only for
non-Christians, but for believers also. Even the most
committed disciples have times when they don't
know how to love Christ. No one understands the
way of God perfectly. Thankfully, we don't have to.

But the more we can understand him, the more we can be like him. And we can come to know his will through his Word and prayer.

Sometimes our question is not, How can I serve God? but simply, What do I do now? Life is full of decisions, great and small, and in those decisions the Lord stands by, waiting for us to ask him to guide us. After his conversion, Saul returns to Jerusalem and receives such guidance:

> When I returned to Jerusalem and was praying at the temple, I fell into a trance and saw the Lord speaking. "Quick!" he said to me. "Leave Jerusalem immediately, because they will not accept your testimony about me."
>
> "Lord," I replied, "these men know that I went from one synagogue to another to imprison and beat those who believe in you. And when the blood of your martyr Stephen was shed, I stood there giving my approval and guarding the clothes of those who were killing him."
>
> Then the Lord said to me, "Go; I will send you far away to the Gentiles" (Acts 22:17-21).

This is an important turning point in Paul's life. He wants to stay in Jerusalem and clear his name. He wants his old friends to know that he now follows this Jesus—the man he once persecuted. But Jesus has other plans for him. He wants to send him to the Gentiles. In prayer, Paul hears Jesus say, "Go."

Like Paul, we, too, make our plans. We decide where to live, what job to have, how to spend our time. Like Paul, we may have valid reasons to stay when Jesus says go. But Paul heard the voice of Jesus in prayer, and he obeyed. Prayer is not just speaking—it is listening.

I'm not convinced we should fall into a trance when we pray. I'm not sure exactly how Jesus speaks to us in prayer. I myself have never heard an audible voice, but wrestling with a decision in prayer, I believe he has answered me and guided me. Sometimes, like Paul, his answer is not what I want to hear, but when we ask God for advice, we should be prepared to take it.

> *Prayer is not just speaking—*
> *it is listening.*

Jesus did not leave us, the church, alone. When we want to know his will, we can read his Word, the Bible, follow the example of his disciples, and listen to his voice in the quiet of prayer. We are not alone as he guides our lives.

Pray with Devotion

In many ways the church in Acts is a model church. However, these early Christians were not perfect. They bickered and fought. Their faith wavered. There were hypocrites in their midst. But most of them held firmly to their faith, even in the face of persecution. They were devoted to God and to one another. Most of all, they were a praying church, calling on their Father time and time again for courage, forgiveness, and guidance. We, too, are called to be praying Christians, completely dependent on God through Christ.

What makes for a good church today? Is the best church the one with the most dynamic preacher? The most programs? The largest attendance? Do we measure a church by the excitement of its members?

By the size of its parking lot? By its reputation in
the community?

No. The truest measure of a church is its devotion
to God. Nothing reflects that devotion more than
prayer. If we lack the spirituality, the boldness, and
the power of the early church, perhaps our prayer
life is the first thing we can change. We must learn
to pray with spirit for the Spirit, and that Spirit will
empower and embolden us.

Focusing Your Faith:

1. What is your church doing regularly to show it really believes in the healing power of prayer?

2. Whenever you or a loved one is ill, whose prayers in particular do you ask for? Why do you think his or her prayers for healing are more effective than others'?

3. Look up these verses about the Holy Spirit: John 14:16, 17, 26; Romans 8:26. How does he help you pray?

4. How do you allow the Holy Spirit to work in your life? How do you hold him back?

5. Think about your most "unforgivable sin." How has God shown you he's forgiven you completely? Have you forgiven yourself?

6. Has God ever initiated prayer with you? How?

7. How much time do you spend listening to God? Take only your Bible into a secluded place. With your Bible open, pray. Then spend thirty minutes just listening.

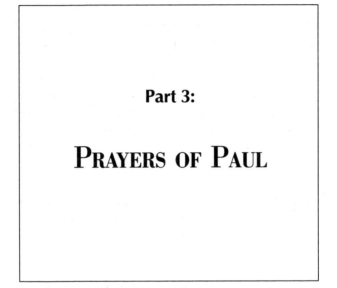

Part 3:

PRAYERS OF PAUL

Chapter 7

Paul Encourages

the Churches

$\mathcal{T}$he religious world has been convinced of the power of prayer for thousands of years. And today even the scientific world is beginning to realize its power. According to Dr. Larry Dossey, author of *Healing Words* (HarperCollins), healing as a result of prayer can be scientifically proven.

Prayer Focus:

Pray with power.

In one study conducted by Dr. Randolph Byrd, a Christian cardiologist, 393 heart patients were divided into two groups—the prayed-for group and the not-prayed-for group. Dr. Byrd then assigned prayer groups to pray for the recovery of the "prayed-for" patients. Each patient had seven to ten people praying for him or her daily. The results were significant: The prayed-for group required fewer antibiotics, were less likely to develop fluid on their lungs, and fewer died.

I don't know if God's power can be confined to a scientific experiment, but I am glad to see scientists finally acknowledging the validity of prayer on the behalf of others.

By looking at Paul's prayers for the churches and his teachings on prayer, we, too, can learn to pray for our brothers and sisters in Christ—for those in our local congregation, in other churches, and even those far away whom we have never met. But more than learning to pray, we can learn what to pray for. Think what could happen if we began praying for the Christians we work with as Paul did. It could revolutionize our lives and ministry together.

Think what could happen if we began praying for the Christians we work with as Paul did.

Paul was probably the most dynamic of the apostles. He was apparently the most prolific writer among them. His letters, written even before the four Gospels, clearly form the theology of the Christian faith. Paul's letters, written with spontaneity, courage, and directness, are full of truth and spiritual teachings that came down from God through the Holy Spirit.

It is no surprise that in light of the Holy Spirit's inspiration, his letters all reflect a spirit of love, affection, and prayer.

In reading Paul's letters many skip over his prayers to get to the "good stuff." For some the good part is Paul's deep presentation of Christian doctrine. His letters are full of profound teachings on redemption, the Holy Spirit, the resurrection, and other doctrines.

For some the good stuff is Paul's advice on Christian living, his comforting words on love, joy, and peace. Paul's letters are indeed a deep reservoir of guidance on Christian living and doctrine, but we can miss both the beauty of discipleship and the significance of doctrine if we ignore his prayers.

When Paul writes a church, he begins by telling them about his prayer for them. This is more than a mere custom of letter composition; by praying, Paul recognizes God the Father and the Lord Jesus as the true correspondents with the church. Their power called the church into existence. Their love binds the church together. Their Spirit gives the church life.

Moreover, Paul's prayers—whether actual prayers or reports of his prayers—usually set the themes for his letters. If you want to know what concerns or encourages him about a particular church, look first to his prayers. There you will find what is on his heart.

Prayer for the Romans—Encouragement

Though he knew many in their number, Paul had never visited the church at Rome. Because this was not a church he had planted, you might expect his letter to them would show less depth of feeling than his other letters. But that is certainly not the case:

First, I thank my God through Jesus Christ for all of you, because your faith is being reported all over the world. God, whom I serve with my whole heart in preaching the gospel of his Son, is my witness how constantly I remember you in my prayers at all times; and I pray that now at last by God's will the way may be opened for me to come to you.

I long to see you so that I may impart to you some spiritual gift to make you strong—that is, that you and I may be mutually encouraged by each other's faith (Romans 1:8-12).

Paul's warm affection for the Romans stems from his knowledge of their faith. So faithful were they that the whole world proclaimed it. Paul prays for them constantly, asking God to bring him to visit them in Rome. The great apostle wants to bring them a spiritual gift, but he also longs to be strengthened by their world-renowned faith.

No matter how strong our faith is or how mature in Christ we become, we always need encouragement from faithful Christians.

Paul's brief prayer for the Romans teaches a lesson in encouragement. He could have stressed his own authority as an apostle—his power to heal and pass on spiritual gifts. He does mention in the letter's opening his call to be an apostle, but in his prayer he prays for mutual encouragement. Paul had learned what truly spiritual disciples always know: No matter how strong our faith is or how mature in Christ we become, we always need encouragement from faithful Christians. Paul certainly knew discouragement; he had endured beatings, stonings, and shipwreck. But when he thought of these faithful Romans, resolute even in adversity, his spirits were brightened.

We may not face persecution as modern Christians, but we certainly face discouragement. Even (perhaps especially) those who publicly lead the church face disappointment and heartbreak. But those of us who lead and teach and preach know we receive more than we give. Examples of ordinary, quiet, but faithful Christians convince us anew of the truth and power of Christianity.

Margaret was such a Christian. A widow, retired from a career in college teaching, her health was somewhat fragile. She couldn't see very well after dark, yet she never missed a church service, even though at times she had to get another church member to drive her. If you had visited our church during Margaret's lifetime, you probably wouldn't have noticed her; she wasn't loud and boisterous, but her acts of quiet service, known only to a few, did not go unnoticed by God.

There are many Margarets in our church and in yours. Such Christians keep my faith alive. Like Paul, I long to meet more of them. Like Paul, we all should pray for opportunities to meet Christian brothers and sisters who will strengthen our faith as we strengthen theirs.

Prayers for the Corinthians

Was there ever a church as mixed-up as the Corinthians? They were proud of their sexual immorality. They were split into quarreling factions. They sued each other in pagan courtrooms. They got drunk during the Lord's Supper. They bragged about their spiritual gifts, but they did not know the way of love.

In short, if there ever was an apostate church—a church gone astray—it was Corinth. How disappointed Paul must have been when he thought of them. He had founded the church at Corinth and spent a year and a half there trying to shape them into disciples of Jesus. As soon as he left, other teachers arrived claiming to know more than Paul and ridiculing his authority. The Corinthians readily followed these "super apostles."

Grace

How do you pray for a church like the one in Corinth? My first inclination would be to pray for God to pay them in kind—to blast them out of the water as they deserve. But that is not Paul's prayer. With all their faults, the Corinthians had received the grace of God. His prayer for them is not one of rebuke, but of thanksgiving:

> I always thank God for you because of his grace given you in Christ Jesus. For in him you have been enriched in every way—in all your speaking and in all your knowledge—because our testimony about Christ was confirmed in you. Therefore you do not lack any spiritual gift as you eagerly wait for our Lord Jesus Christ to be revealed. He will keep you strong to the end, so that you will be blameless on the day of our Lord Jesus Christ. God, who has called you into fellowship with his Son Jesus Christ our Lord, is faithful (1 Corinthians 1:4-9).

Thank God the salvation of the Corinthians was not dependent on their ability to be a model church but on God's gracious act in Jesus Christ. This gracious God gave them their spiritual gifts—faith and knowledge. And this faithful God will present them blameless at the last day.

This does not mean the Corinthians had no reason to repent; in the rest of 1 Corinthians Paul points out their shortcomings and calls them back to faithfulness. They must put away selfish divisions; they must have orderly worship; they must live moral lives based on love. But all these things are by God's grace alone, and for that grace Paul is thankful.

How do we pray for weak, apostate Christians? We may be tempted to pray, "Lord, straighten them out!" Certainly there is a place for such a prayer. Some of our brothers and sisters may need God to figuratively hit them between the eyes to get their attention. But in praying for wayward Christians, we must remember that no matter how sinful they might be, they are our brothers or sisters in Christ. They, too, are saved by the power of God's grace, as are we, and it is that grace that calls them to repentance. Like Paul, we can praise God for even the most disobedient Christian and thank God for his marvelous grace.

Comfort

The tone of 2 Corinthians differs greatly from that of 1 Corinthians. It appears the Corinthians have repented of many of the wrongs they had committed, so Paul prays that God will console them:

> Praise be to the God and Father of our Lord Jesus Christ, the Father of compassion and the God of all comfort, who comforts us in all our troubles, so that we can comfort those in any trouble with the comfort we ourselves have received from God. For just as the sufferings of Christ flow over into our lives, so also through Christ our comfort overflows. If we are distressed, it is for your comfort and salvation; if we are comforted, it is for your comfort, which produces in you patient endurance of the same sufferings we suffer. And our hope for you is firm, because we know that just as you share in our sufferings, so also you share in our comfort (2 Corinthians 1:3-7).

Talk about repeating yourself, Paul uses *comfort* nine times in these five verses. Why did the Corinthians need to be consoled? One reason was their sorrow for their sins. Paul had written them a strong letter, calling the sincerity of their faith into question. Even in this letter he urges them to test their faith to see if it is genuine (2 Corinthians 13:5). When confronted by sin, the faithful Christian responds with a godly sorrow that leads to repentance. This is more than merely saying we're sorry; to repent is to realize we have offended the holy God and have hurt Jesus himself, the one who died for us. Such sorrow cuts deep into the soul and can only be removed by the consolation of God's forgiveness.

To repent is to realize we have
offended the holy God and have hurt
Jesus himself, the one who died for us.

Paul knew that affliction produces patient endurance of suffering. And he knew the Corinthians certainly needed consolation in their affliction. If there was anyone who knew suffering and pain, it was Paul. If there was anyone who knew the comfort of God in the midst of pain, it was Paul. As the Father comforted the Son in his agony, so he consoled Paul, who in turn shared the comfort of God with the Corinthians.

Thankfully, I have not faced much physical affliction for my faith, but I have known sickness, pain, and injury. While writing this chapter, I broke my elbow. I'd like to claim some noble reason for my pain, but the fact is I broke it playing softball. For the three long weeks my right arm was in a cast, I

couldn't write, mow the grass, or even feed myself
easily. During this time, the church gave me a
surprise birthday party, and one brother endeared
himself to me forever by cutting my piece of cake
into bite-sized pieces. Such was my "great suffering."
But as minor as it was, I needed consolation from my
fellow Christians and from God, and I got it. In
troubles small and great, God is our consolation, and
he expects us to console others.

Most of our suffering is not a result of our Christian faith. Suffering for Christ seems far removed
from our experience as modern Christians. In the
fifties being a good church member advanced, not
hindered, our standing in our jobs and in our community. But times have definitely changed. We no
longer live in a Christian America. In most places,
being a dedicated Christian will not help you socially
or on the job. For most in our society Christianity is
still tolerable "as long as you don't take it too far."
But that is precisely what we are called to do—to go
too far, to give our all to Christ. No, we don't have to
be objectionable just to be so, but if we have the
mind of Christ and live our lives for him, some will
object, perhaps even violently. We, too, may come to
know the need for God's comfort in persecution.

We also need comfort when facing loss. While
writing this I participated in the funeral of one of
our church members. Russell Cooper had been a
faithful leader in our church. A few years ago he had
a series of strokes that left him severely incapaci-
tated. Each day for years his wife Myrtie faithfully
visited Russell in the nursing home and cared for
him. She consoled him with God's consolation. When
Russell passed away, I was asked to read Scripture
and pray at his funeral. Ostensibly, I was there to
comfort Myrtie, but it was her giving, undying love

that was the true consolation to me and to all those around her.

The Corinthians had lost loved ones too. Some were beginning to doubt the resurrection. They thought they would never see their loved ones again. In 1 Corinthians 15 Paul had written them to assure them that death would be swallowed up in victory. As we stood by Russell's grave, I thought of those comforting words.

Perfection

Suffering, sin, and death. Three strong foes of faith. Paul knew the Corinthians could crack under their pressure, so at the end of this letter he says another prayer for them, a prayer for their perfection:

> Now we pray to God that you will not do anything wrong. Not that people will see that we have stood the test but that you will do what is right even though we may seem to have failed. For we cannot do anything against the truth, but only for the truth. We are glad whenever we are weak but you are strong; and our prayer is for your perfection. This is why I write these things when I am absent, that when I come I may not have to be harsh in my use of authority—the authority the Lord gave me for building you up, not for tearing you down (2 Corinthians 13:7-10).

Paul's final words sound ominous, but in the context of prayer we find their true intent. Paul is not an authoritarian dictator but a loving father in the gospel. Even if he fails, he wants the Corinthians to pass the test of faith, so he calls on the only power that can make them pass. He calls on God in prayer.

Suffering, sin—including indifference, materialism, and pride—and death are our enemies too. If our faith is to pass the test, we also must rely on God in prayer. And we must pray for each other. If Paul could ask God to perfect a church as weak as the one in Corinth, then we can pray for our weakest brothers or sisters. And they can pray for us.

Prayer for the Ephesians—Knowledge

Knowledge is power. At least that is what we are told in today's information age. When writing to the Ephesians, Paul prays they will receive a different sort of knowledge and power:

> I have not stopped giving thanks for you, remembering you in my prayers. I keep asking that the God of our Lord Jesus Christ, the glorious Father, may give you the Spirit of wisdom and revelation, so that you may know him better. I pray also that the eyes of your heart may be enlightened in order that you may know the hope to which he has called you, the riches of his glorious inheritance in the saints, and his incomparably great power for us who believe (Ephesians 1:16-19).

Knowledge of God is much more than a theological education. I do not want to disparage Christian education; I've been in that business all my life. But knowing about God is not the same as knowing God. Knowing the Bible is important. We should teach it to our children, take time to study it ourselves, and insist our church leaders get the very best biblical education they can get. But book knowledge about someone, even from the best Book, is not the same as knowing that person. God surely wants us to learn about him, but most of all he wants us to know him.

I know many things about my wife Deb: her taste in clothes, her favorite color, the foods she likes, her sense of humor. But passing a quiz on her tastes and habits does not qualify me as a good husband or ensure a good marriage. What makes our marriage good is that we know one another. We are part of each other. We think and feel together. God calls us to have this same kind of intimate knowledge of him. Paul prays that the Ephesians will receive not simply intellectual information, but that "the eyes of your heart may be enlightened." Our Father wants us to see him with the eyes of our heart. Can there be a more intimate knowledge?

> *Our Father wants us to see him*
> *with the eyes of our heart.*

Such knowledge is a gift from God. Yes, we must strain every nerve to know our Father, but we can only know him when we look for him to reveal himself to us. Paul prays that God "may give you the Spirit of wisdom and revelation, so that you may know him better." If we want to know God better, we need only to ask him. Do you want to improve your Bible study? Then coat your studies with prayer. Knowledge and wisdom come through prayer. Ask God to give you wisdom as you study his Word and pray that he will reveal himself to you fully. It is in prayer that we come to know the Father intimately, and it is in prayer that he grants us even fuller knowledge.

Who is this God we come to know? He is the God who gives hope, "the riches of his glorious inherit-ance in the saints." The more we come to know him, the more we come to realize what he has done for us. When we were hopeless, he gave us hope. When we

were orphans, he adopted us and made us heirs.
Today our world is low on hope. Cynicism abounds.
The things on which we place our hope prove futile:
wealth, technology, democracy, family, pleasure, and
others. God alone is the source of true hope. His is a
true and sure hope, not just a fond wish for things to
get better. The more we come to know our Father,
the clearer we see the reality of our inheritance. We
have begun to live with him forever.

To know God is to have power over temptation, sin, evil, and Satan.

Knowledge is power. The God we come to know is
a powerful God. The same power that raised Christ
from the dead, that placed him in the heavens, and
that appointed him head over the church is the same
power that is at work in us (Ephesians 1:20-23). To
know God is to have power over temptation, sin, evil,
and Satan. To know God is to have power over every
situation we face each day. To know God is to have
the power of Christ in us, the Christ who fills us in
every way.

Knowledge is power. Paul repeats that in his
second prayer for the Ephesians:

> For this reason I kneel before the Father, from
> whom his whole family in heaven and on earth
> derives its name. I pray that out of his glorious
> riches he may strengthen you with power through
> his Spirit in your inner being so that Christ may
> dwell in your hearts through faith. And I pray
> that you, being rooted and established in love,
> may have power, together with all the saints, to
> grasp how wide and long and high and deep is the

love of Christ, and to know this love that surpasses knowledge—that you may be filled to the measure of all the fullness of God (Ephesians 3:14-19).

Knowledge of God brings power, but here Paul turns it around—he prays the Ephesians will have the power to know. To know what? To know the essence of Christ—the extent of his love. Yet that love is really beyond knowledge, we can't imagine how wide and long and high and deep it is. But as we come to know our God and our Christ, we grasp more and more the love that they are. That love fills us and spills from us to all we meet.

The only way to understand God's love is to ask him for the ability to understand. When we do, we will be filled to the measure of all the fullness of Christ. We cannot be filled to the measure until we have an understanding of God's love. And we're not given that knowledge until we ask for it in prayer. So prayer is directly related to our maturity in Christ. To pray is to grow, to change.

Do you want to know God? Then pray. Ask to know him. Do you sometimes feel hopeless? Then pray. Ask to know the sure hope he calls us to. Are you sometimes powerless against the forces arrayed against you? Pray for power. Power to overcome. Power to know the love of Christ. Do not face your problems on your own. Use your power to encourage others. Power is yours. All you have to do is ask.

Focusing Your Faith:

1. If prayer is the starting point for maturity in Christ, what is your church doing now to grow spiritually?

2. How can you praise God for the most disobedient Christians you know? How can you help the Lord comfort them?

3. Looking with the "eyes of your heart," what new thing do you know about God?

4. How does knowing God give *you* the power of Christ? How does it change your approach to daily problems?

5. How has knowing God caused you to treat the people you work/associate with differently from the way they treat you?

6. Write a note of encouragement to one of your congregation's missionaries.

7. Conduct your own "scientific experiment" with prayer. Pray every day for the healing or encouragement of someone you know. Record his or her condition at the end of each week.

Chapter 8

Paul Praises
the Churches

$\mathcal{T}$he old preacher stood up to preach. He read from Matthew 4:24, ". . . they brought unto him all sick people that were taken with divers diseases."

The preacher shouted, "Now, the doctors can scrutinize

Prayer Focus:

Pray with faith.

you, analyze you, and sometimes cure your ills, but when you have divers diseases, then only the Lord can cure. And folks, there is a regular epidemic of divers diseases among us.

"Some of you dive for the door after Sunday school is over. Some of you dive for the TV set after church. Some dive into a list of excuses about not working for the Lord. Others dive for the car and take a trip over the weekend. Some dive for their nickels and dimes to put into the offering, instead of tithing. Some dive for the door as soon as the minister gives the appeal to respond to the invitation. Yes, but the Lord loves this church, even with its divers diseases, and he can cure you."

I've been very blessed; I've never been part of a church with "divers diseases." Every church I've experienced has been full of people who give of themselves fully and freely, who show love to the downtrodden, and who express the true joy of God. Oh sure, there have been occasional church members who gossip, lie, and cheat, but they have been rare in my church experience.

So how do you pray for a faithful church? What do you say about Christians whose lives seem much more exemplary than your own? Paul knew such a church, and he knew how to pray for them.

Prayer for the Philippians—Love

Every church has its problems and its strong points, but if there is one church in the New Testament that can be described as an exceptional church, it is the church at Philippi. When Paul writes to the Philippians, the tone of his letter is completely positive with lavish praise for them. He sets this tone in his prayer for the Philippians:

> I thank my God every time I remember you. In all my prayers for all of you, I always pray with joy because of your partnership in the gospel from the first day until now, being confident of this, that he who began a good work in you will carry it on to completion until the day of Christ Jesus. . . . And this is my prayer: that your love may abound more and more in knowledge and depth of insight, so that you may be able to discern what is best and may be pure and blameless until the day

of Christ, filled with the fruit of righteousness
that comes through Jesus Christ—to the glory
and praise of God (Philippians 1:3-6, 9-11).

Paul's prayers for the Philippians are prayers of
joy. He introduces the central themes of this letter—
joy and rejoicing—in his prayer. Paul rejoices over
the way the Philippians share in the gospel. They
had gladly received the gospel as the saving truth
from God. More than that, they had supported Paul's
proclamation of the gospel through their generous
gifts and their prayers. Yet this good work was not
their own doing, it was begun by Christ, and Paul
prays he will bring it to completion at the last day.

_**Knowing God changes the
way we think, the way we live,
the way we treat others.**_

Paul's prayer for the Philippians is quite similar
to his prayer for the Corinthians and the Ephesians.
As with the Ephesians, he wants God to grant them
love and knowledge. Paul wanted the Ephesians to
know the love of God; he wants the Philippians' love
to overflow with knowledge. In Christianity, love and
knowledge go hand in hand. To know God is to love
him. When we love him, we come to know him more
and more.

This knowledge of God is more than simply an
intellectual achievement. Knowing God changes the
way we think, the way we live, the way we treat
others. As Paul prayed for the Corinthians, so he
prays for the Philippians that this God they have
come to know and love will produce good lives, a
"harvest of righteousness," that they may be pure

and blameless on the day of Christ.

Is this the way we pray for our fellow Christians? It seems most of our prayers are for people to be healed or comforted. These are certainly commendable prayers. As Paul prayed for his brothers and sisters to be healed or consoled, he was primarily concerned with their standing before God. Using Paul's prayer, the church today can learn to pray for what is most important: that we and our fellow Christians may know the love of God and may live blameless lives, looking forward to that final endless day of Jesus Christ.

Prayer for the Colossians—Hope

It is not surprising for Paul to repeat himself in his prayers for the different churches. After all, most churches face the same struggles and share the same joys. Though Paul's actual prayers are not recorded, his reports of his prayers are. If we could actually have heard Paul pray for the churches, we would probably find his prayers were personalized to fit each congregation.

When we come to Paul's prayer for the Colossian church, we find little that is new. Paul wrote to the Colossians about the same time as to the Ephesians, and the two letters are quite similar. Paul's prayer for the Colossians, therefore, echoes many of the themes of his other prayers:

> We always thank God, the Father of our Lord Jesus Christ, when we pray for you, because we have heard of your faith in Christ Jesus and of the love you have for all the saints—the faith and love that spring from the hope that is stored up for you in heaven and that you have already heard about in the word of truth, the gospel. . . .

For this reason, since the day we heard about you, we have not stopped praying for you and asking God to fill you with the knowledge of his will through all spiritual wisdom and understanding. And we pray this in order that you may live a life worthy of the Lord and may please him in every way: bearing fruit in every good work, growing in the knowledge of God, being strengthened with all power according to his glorious might so that you may have great endurance and patience, and joyfully giving thanks to the Father, who has qualified you to share in the inheritance of the saints in the kingdom of light (Colossians 1:3-5, 9-12).

Here is Paul's usual prayer vocabulary. He thanks God for the church's faith, hope, and love, and prays for them to receive the knowledge that brings good works, strength, and endurance. The new terms he emphasizes to the Colossians are *hope* and *endurance*, perhaps reflecting the sufferings of the church or of Paul himself, since he wrote this from prison (Colossians 4:10). In either case, endurance is needed. The power to endure springs from one of the greatest doctrines of Christianity: the hope waiting for us in heaven.

The Bible's definition of hope is the complete opposite of the way we usually use the word. In everyday use, to hope is to wish fondly for something—"I hope it doesn't rain today," "I hope the boss gives me a raise," "I hope little Johnny is all right," —wishes with varying degrees of certainty about their outcome. In the Scriptures hope is a sure thing, because it is based not on our own actions but on the gracious act of God in Jesus Christ.

Growing up as a Christian, I remember several

occasions when older Christians were asked, "If you died today, would you go to heaven?" Almost invariably they answered, "I hope so," in much the same tone they used to say, "I hope it doesn't rain today." The one exception was an elderly woman in our church who promptly replied, "Yes, I know I'd go to heaven." When asked how she could be so sure, she said simply, "God told me I was saved, and I believe him." That lady knew the true meaning of Christian hope. Didn't Christ say, "I go to prepare a place for you"? Didn't he pray that we should share his glory? If we believe him, our hope is sure.

Certainty of hope moves Christians to loving action for God and for neighbor.

But the hope of heaven is much more than "pie in the sky when you die by and by." Our hope is waiting for us in heaven, but it also guides our present lives. Some fear that assurance of salvation and certainty of hope will lead Christians to neglect their service to Christ. If we already have it made, why put ourselves out? Paul sees hope in a different light. He thanks God for the Colossians' hope because it motivates their faith in Christ and their love for the saints. Hope in their inheritance gives them power to endure. Certainty of hope moves Christians to loving action for God and for neighbor.

What has all of this to do with prayer? We, too, can thank God for the hope within us and the hope we see in fellow Christians. What is more, hope forms the context for every prayer we pray. We could not pray without our hope of being heard. We could not pray, "Your will be done," if we had no sure hope that God's will would lead ultimately to our personal triumph over evil. His will is for us to be saved. We always pray with confidence. We always pray in hope.

Prayers for the Thessalonians

The Thessalonian letters are probably the earliest letters of Paul, yet they already contain his distinctive prayer vocabulary:

We always thank God for all of you, mentioning you in our prayers. We continually remember before our God and Father your work produced by faith, your labor prompted by love, and your endurance inspired by hope in our Lord Jesus Christ (1 Thessalonians 1:2, 3).

Faith, hope, love—Paul's three favorite words. This is what he thanks God for. But these are more than theological terms for Paul, more than just church words to be used on Sunday. They are action words. He thanks God for their work of faith. True faith always shows itself in action, in work for God and others. Paul thanks God for their labor of love. Love is no good if it is love in name only. Love expresses itself in serving others. Paul thanks God for their steadfastness of hope. Hope is not mere wishful thinking, but a sure hope that inspires endurance. To Paul, faith, hope, and love are more than virtues; they always lead to ethical action. They are gifts from God and causes for thanksgiving.

Holiness

Later in 1 Thessalonians we have both an account of Paul's prayers for the church in Thessalonica and an actual prayer:

How can we thank God enough for you in return

for all the joy we have in the presence of our God because of you? Night and day we pray most earnestly that we may see you again and supply what is lacking in your faith.

Now may our God and Father himself and our Lord Jesus clear the way for us to come to you. May the Lord make your love increase and overflow for each other and for everyone else, just as ours does for you. May he strengthen your hearts so that you will be blameless and holy in the presence of our God and Father when our Lord Jesus comes with all his holy ones (1 Thessalonians 3:9-13).

Paul is so overwhelmed with the joy he feels when he thinks of the Thessalonians, that he breaks out in blessing. Thankful to God for that joy, he asks him to increase their love and to make them holy and blameless.

How often do we pray for holiness today? *Holiness* itself carries overtones of hypocrisy or fanaticism, but it is essential to our Christian character. To be genuinely holy is not to be "holier than thou" but rather is God's action of transforming us into the image of Christ. Holiness is no option for Christians; we are made holy to stand blameless before God at the coming of Jesus. This holiness is not the result of our own spiritual fervor or discipline, it is a gift of God—a gift to be sought in prayer. It is God who sanctifies us, who disciplines us, and who presents us blameless. As Paul prayed for the Thessalonians, so we can pray for God to strengthen our hearts in holiness.

Worthiness

In his second letter, Paul repeats his thanksgiving

and requests for the Thessalonian church:

> We ought always to thank God for you, brothers, and rightly so, because your faith is growing more and more, and the love every one of you has for each other is increasing.

> With this in mind, we constantly pray for you, that our God may count you worthy of his calling, and that by his power he may fulfill every good purpose of yours and every act prompted by your faith. We pray this so that the name of our Lord Jesus may be glorified in you, and you in him, according to the grace of our God and the Lord Jesus Christ (2 Thessalonians 1:3, 11, 12).

Again he is thankful for their faith and prays for God to empower their work of faith. He also prays that God will make them worthy of his call. Here is a look backward and a look forward. We Christians look back to the moment God called us from a life of sin and we obeyed that call (2 Thessalonians 2:13, 14). At that moment no one was worthy; we all were sinners without hope, yet God called us to eternal life. Thus we look forward to the coming of our Lord (2 Thessalonians 1:9-12). Between the time of our calling and the time of our glory, God works in us to make us worthy of his call. For that we pray and praise him for his glorious grace.

Prayer for Timothy—Nurtured Faith

Paul wrote letters to individuals as well as to churches. These letters reveal Paul's love and appreciation for their working to share their faith with others. He praises Timothy and Philemon for the encouragement he receives from their efforts.

Gratitude for his fellow Christians marked Paul's

life, and he is especially thankful for Timothy. Paul calls him "my true son in the faith" and says:

> I thank God, whom I serve, as my forefathers did, with a clear conscience, as night and day I constantly remember you in my prayers. Recalling your tears, I long to see you, so that I may be filled with joy. I have been reminded of your sincere faith, which first lived in your grandmother Lois and in your mother Eunice and, I am persuaded, now lives in you also (2 Timothy 1:3-5).

Since Timothy's father was Greek (and by implication an unbeliever), Paul became Timothy's surrogate father. Timothy is blessed by two influential women in his life, Lois and Eunice, in whom sincere faith lived. Paul is thankful for these women, and particularly thankful for Timothy's love for them and him. Timothy's tears stand as a witness of his love for Paul.

"Faith of our fathers, holy faith," we sometimes sing. But what about the faith of our mothers? For Timothy and for many of us, it was a faithful mother or grandmother who first taught us of Jesus. Some of my earliest memories are of Mom tucking me into bed and reading me a Bible story. A few days ago I heard a song she sometimes sang to me, and I unexpectedly burst into tears. Such memories are precious. Few of us come to faith on our own; our faith is nurtured, sometimes through great effort and sacrifice, by our families. We also have the responsibility and joy of passing the faith on to our children and our grandchildren. What a rich heritage!

We, too, have the privilege of living out our faith before the eyes of our children. To possess a faithful mother, grandmother, father, brother, sister, and child is a great boon from God. In prayer we, like

Paul, thank him for those whose lives bless ours.

Prayer for Philemon—Shared Faith

This faith we have from our families is not a precious commodity to be hoarded. It is a precious commodity that should be shared. Paul writes Philemon and rejoices, praising him for sharing his faith with others:

> I always thank my God as I remember you in my prayers, because I hear about your faith in the Lord Jesus and your love for all the saints. I pray that you may be active in sharing your faith, so that you will have a full understanding of every good thing we have in Christ. Your love has given me great joy and encouragement, because you, brother, have refreshed the hearts of the saints (Philemon 4-7).

Sharing your faith can mean evangelism, and that may be what Paul has in mind here. However, we also share our faith with fellow Christians, refreshing their hearts. To share faith also means to do good for Christ. In Philemon's case, doing good meant receiving and forgiving Onesimus, his runaway slave.

Share the faith. This brief phrase summarizes the whole of the Christian life. If our faith is genuine, we will tell others the good news of Jesus. Our faith will encourage the hearts of the faithful. And our faith will lead us to good works, even to accept and forgive those who harm us. We thank God for our faith and the faith of others, and we pray for courage to actively share that faith.

Focusing Your Faith:

1. Whom do you credit for nurturing your faith?

2. What person do you consider a model Christian? What do you pray for him or her?

3. Who is praying for your faith, hope, and endurance? If you don't know of anyone, ask someone to pray for you.

4. Who are you praying for daily (in addition to family members) for faith, hope, and endurance?

5. How often do you pray for holiness?

6. Do you believe you are going to heaven if you die today? Why or why not?

7. When was the last time you refreshed someone's heart by sharing your faith? Plan to share your faith at least once a day for the next two weeks.

Chapter 9

Coming Together
to Pray

$\mathcal{A}$ second grader was trying out for the school play. After he left for school, his mother began to worry. What if he didn't get a part? How could she heal his disappointment?

When the mother picked him up at school, he bounded into the car with great enthusiasm.

Prayer Focus:

Pray with thanksgiving.

"Guess what!" he said. "I got the part in the school play!"

"Wonderful!" his mom said. "What part did you get?"

With pride bursting from his face, he replied, "I was picked to clap and cheer!"

Sometimes in prayer we must clap and cheer. God is good! We are blessed! Our hearts burst with the joy of his gifts. That's the way Paul prayed, and that's what he taught the early church. Prayer is not just for asking, it's also for thanking.

Give Thanks

Praising and thanking God for his marvelous gifts is prayer's true essence. Paul frequently reminds his readers that thanksgiving is a necessary part of prayer. He models this spirit of thanksgiving by breaking out in prayer in the middle of his letters. For example, in the middle of a discussion of the contribution for the Christians in Judea he says, "I thank God, who put into the heart of Titus the same concern I have for you" (2 Corinthians 8:16). Titus's concern for the Corinthians did not spring from himself; it was the gift of God. To Paul any attitude that promoted the spread of the gospel and led to unity among Christians was a gift of God. Today we need the same faith to see spiritual growth in the church as a gift of God. Like Paul, we should be thankful for that gift.

Sing with Gratitude

At times our hearts are so full of the joy of thanksgiving that we cannot express it with words alone. At those times, lifting our voices in song more fully expresses our gratitude.

Let the peace of Christ rule in your hearts, since as members of one body you were called to peace. And be thankful. Let the word of Christ dwell in you richly as you teach and admonish one another with all wisdom, and as you sing psalms, hymns and spiritual songs with gratitude in your hearts to God. And whatever you do, whether in word or deed, do it all in the name of the Lord Jesus, giving thanks to God the Father through him (Colossians 3:15-17).

Singing does many things for the Christian. Christ's word dwells within us as we sing. We teach and encourage one another in song. Most importantly, we praise our holy God in song, singing with gratitude in our hearts for all he has done for us. These songs of thanksgiving are also prayers to him. In Ephesians 5:18-20 Paul also speaks of singing. He tells the Ephesians to be filled with the Spirit and speak to each other in songs, but also to sing and make music in their hearts to the Lord, always giving thanks to God in Jesus' name.

> *Paul simply realized that true thankfulness is not an emotion but an attitude.*

But what if we don't feel like singing? What if we've had a terrible day? What if we can't find anything to be thankful for? The Bible encourages us to sing anyway. Sing and pray even when you don't feel like it. Be thankful even in trouble. As Paul says, ". . . always giving thanks to God the Father for everything, in the name of our Lord Jesus Christ" (Ephesians 5:20).

How can we be thankful at all times? How can we sing with gratitude when we don't feel it? Is Paul demanding the impossible, or is he advocating hypocrisy? Does he want us to fake our gratitude when we are not in the mood to be genuinely grateful?

None of the above. Paul simply realized that true thankfulness is not an emotion but an attitude. Paul himself certainly did not always feel like thanking God. Stoned, shipwrecked, beaten, imprisoned, and even given a thorn in the flesh, he knew suffering and pain firsthand, yet he could give thanks at all times and for all things. How? Because of faith. He trusted God to bring good out of evil, blessing out of suffering. He knew his current pains could not be compared with the glory he would receive. That's how he and Silas could sing praises from a prison cell (Acts 16:25).

Count It All Joy!

So are we to thank God for the trouble that comes upon us? Can we honestly thank God for broken bones, for terminal diseases, for the loss of our loved ones? No. We must remember our loving Father does not send evil. Paul's thorn in the flesh was from Satan, not from God (2 Corinthians 12:7). The Lord did not remove the thorn, but he used that evil as an occasion to give grace (v. 9). We are not thankful for trouble, but we can thank God for everything that happens to us when we trust him to suffer with us and transform our pain into glory. And that is precisely what he has promised.

When suffering, don't stop praying—Christ will help you find some way to be thankful to God.

Thus Paul can say, "Be joyful always; pray continually; give thanks in all circumstances, for this is God's will for you in Christ Jesus" (1 Thessalonians 5:16-18). God's will is for us to learn contentment with the things we have and with everything that happens (Philippians 4:11). No matter what horrors we face in life, we can be courageous like Paul because we can do all things through the strength Christ gives us (Philippians 4:13). When suffering, don't stop praying—Christ will help you find some way to be thankful to God.

Our salvation is one thing we can always thank God for. When trouble comes we know God still loves us because he sent his Son to save us.

> I thank Christ Jesus our Lord, who has given me strength, that he considered me faithful, appointing me to his service. Even though I was once a blasphemer and a persecutor and a violent man, I was shown mercy because I acted in ignorance and unbelief. The grace of our Lord was poured out on me abundantly, along with the faith and love that are in Christ Jesus.
>
> Here is a trustworthy saying that deserves full acceptance: Christ Jesus came into the world to save sinners—of whom I am the worst (1 Timothy 1:12-15).

Paul could withstand any hardship because God saved him, the foremost of sinners, even though he was on the road to Damascus to kill more Christians. Paul never forgot he was a sinner, but neither did he forget the grace of God. So he could be grateful to God no matter what came his way.

Today trouble comes to us and threatens to overwhelm. My good friend found out that his fourteen-year-old daughter had cancer. She bravely fought through months of chemotherapy, weight loss, and discouragement. Afterwards my wife visited with them and found that the prognosis was good. Just one month later we learned this courageous girl would have her leg amputated. I can only imagine the anguish this family feels. We cry in pain wondering how a loving God could allow this to happen to his children—*to our children*. But we have power to overcome our pain, doubts, and fears. Our salvation is sure. Because God loves us, he offers us grace. Because of his grace, we can accept our salvation and thank God for it. If he gave his own Son for us, will he not give us all we need? Surely we can rejoice in his promises. And for that we are always thankful.

Praying Together

There are times for us to pray alone, times for us to pray with a few fellow Christians, and there are also times for the whole church to pray together. These public prayers take place each time we assemble. Christian assemblies in the first century were quite different from ours in several ways, but they always included corporate prayer to God. The Corinthian church had severe problems in their worship—drunkenness at the Lord's Supper, divisions in the assembly, confusion when several spoke in tongues or prophesied at the same time—so Paul writes them concerning propriety in worship and public prayer:

> Every man who prays or prophesies with his head covered dishonors his head. And every woman who prays or prophesies with her head uncovered dishonors her head—it is just as though her head were shaved.

> Judge for yourselves: Is it proper for a woman to pray to God with her head uncovered? Does not the very nature of things teach you that if a man has long hair, it is a disgrace to him, but that if a woman has long hair, it is her glory? For long hair is given to her as a covering. If anyone wants to be contentious about this, we have no other

practice—nor do the churches of God (1 Corinthians 11:4, 5, 13-16).

Let's consider what this passage has to say to the modern church concerning prayer.

Prayer Leaders

One teaching on public prayer clearly comes through. Paul assumes both men and women will pray when the church comes together. Does this mean women may lead prayer? I'm not sure. Leading prayer is a fairly modern church practice. In Corinth, it appears that different individuals as moved by the Holy Spirit would pray out loud in the assembly. Thus a man or a woman might pray aloud. Paul is not attempting to keep women from praying, but he does want to make sure both women and men wear acceptable cultural dress and have a proper motivation for speaking out.

Women as well as men need to pray in church. Of course, when someone leads in prayer, all Christians in the assembly, whether male or female, pray with the leader. Paul may be saying more than that. There are times when several Christians should raise their voices to God in prayer, one at a time, and some of those voices might be feminine. Our churches might be stronger if we heard our brothers and sisters pray aloud. This does not mean all distinctions between men and women disappear in church, for the primary purpose of this passage is to dispel that notion. But we must remember that women, no less than men, are heirs of salvation and have a Father who hears their prayers.

Prayer Language

Paul's second concern with public prayer in

Corinth is that it be understandable. Several
Corinthians could speak in tongues; they could pray
in a special language. Such prayer was helpful in
private. But in public assemblies of the church when
the prayer was not interpreted and understood, it
did not build up other Christians and confused the
outsider.

> For if I pray in a tongue, my spirit prays, but my
> mind is unfruitful. So what shall I do? I will pray
> with my spirit, but I will also pray with my mind;
> I will sing with my spirit, but I will also sing with
> my mind. If you are praising God with your spirit,
> how can one who finds himself among those who
> do not understand say "Amen" to your thanksgiv-
> ing, since he does not know what you are saying?
> You may be giving thanks well enough, but the
> other man is not edified.

> I thank God that I speak in tongues more than all
> of you. But in the church I would rather speak five
> intelligible words to instruct others than ten thou-
> sand words in a tongue (1 Corinthians 14:14-19).

This passage indicates that even if one can speak
in tongues, there is no place for the gift in public
prayer. Prayer with other Christians must be understandable. All must be able to say "Amen" to the
prayer. The principle that public prayer must be
understandable applies to all churches. Tongues are
not the only obstacle to understanding prayer.
Mumbling, using an unfamiliar vocabulary, slipping
into a strange "prayer tone," and praying only for
personal situations can all make for obscure public
prayers. It's vital that we communicate clearly when
we pray publicly since others are praying with us.
We must even consider the outsiders who come to

our assembly. Our public worship should not confuse or offend them. If they are offended, it should not be because we have led confusing prayers.

Prayer Focus

Public prayer is aimed in two directions at once. The focus of every prayer is God; he is the only one to whom we speak in prayer. Public prayer is not a lecture forum or a mini-sermon. At the same time we pray to God, we are aware of our fellow Christians, for we pray together. It is our joint prayers that ascend to the Father. Like private prayer, public prayer addresses our audience of one, God, but it must also build up our brothers and sisters.

What kinds of prayers should be offered in public? For whom should we pray? How should we pray? Paul helps us with these questions in 1 Timothy.

First of all, then, I urge that supplications, prayers, intercessions, and thanksgivings be made for everyone, for kings and all who are in high positions, so that we may lead a quiet and peaceable life in all godliness and dignity. . . .

I desire, then, that in every place the men should pray, lifting up holy hands without anger or argument (1 Timothy 2:1, 2, 8, NRSV).

Four words are used here to describe prayer:

1. *Supplications* are heartfelt requests to God for help through personal difficulty.

2. *Prayer* also implies our requests to God, but in a broader sense of asking for his care in all circumstances.

3. *Intercessions* are prayers for others. We petition God on behalf of our brothers,

sisters, and neighbors.

4. *Thanksgivings* spring from our changed
hearts in gratitude for God's gifts.

These terms do not so much describe four separate types of prayer, but point to elements found in
most public prayers. When we come together we
make requests to God for ourselves and for others,
and we thank him for his blessings.

We pray such prayers for everyone, but particularly for kings and those in high positions. In Paul's
day many rulers persecuted Christians, yet Christians are told to pray even for unjust rulers in hope
that God will make ungodly kings leave believers in
peace. Our God is so powerful he can work through
evil rulers to accomplish his purposes. No matter
what kind of government rules us, we still pray the
authorities will allow us quiet and peaceable Christian lives.

Prayer Posture

As far as how to pray, the phrase "lifting up holy
hands" prompts the question of bodily posture in
prayer. The Bible gives many positions for prayer:
standing, kneeling, bowing the face to the ground,
lifting hands, and others. No one position is promoted as the only proper way of praying. In public or
private prayer we may kneel or bow or stand or raise
hands. What we may not do is criticize a brother or
sister who prays in a position that is different from
ours. Neither should we adopt an unusual prayer
position for the purpose of self-gratification or attention. Our church's custom should affect our practice.
Public prayer is a time for Christians to be united in
their petitions to God. It is not a time (indeed, there
is never an acceptable time) for us to bicker and

argue over how we pray. Our hearts, not our posture, determine the genuineness of our prayers.

Our hearts, not our posture, determine
the genuineness of our prayers.

Having said this, it does appear to me that our posture says something about our attitude in prayer. In the Old Testament, it was common to throw oneself face downward in prayer to express respect for the Almighty. In my own boyhood I remember how sincerely impressed I was to see men and women kneeling in prayer. Too much can be made of "body language," but I can't help wondering why we stopped kneeling: was it the inconvenience, pride, or a lack of reverence?

Whatever our posture or whoever is praying, something special happens when the church praises God together in song and prayer. The routine of our public worship may blind us to the beauty of corporate prayer. In a world where most look out for number one, Christians put aside their differences and join together to approach their Father in thanksgiving and to encourage each other. What could be more beautiful this side of heaven?

Focusing Your Faith:

1. Whose prayers do you most enjoy hearing? Why? Whose prayers inspire you most?

2. What could be done to improve public prayer in your church?

3. What prayer song best expresses your feelings today: "I Need Thee Every Hour," "I Just Want to Thank You," or "Answer My Prayer"?

4. When do you feel most listened to by God—when you're praying in private or in public? Why?

5. In what position do you feel most comfortable praying when you're alone? In what position do you feel closest to God? Most reverent?

6. What are you most thankful for? What are you most troubled by? Spend time in prayer thanking God for both.

7. How do you show your thanks to God when you are most grateful? What do you think is God's favorite way of being thanked?

Chapter 10

One
in the Spirit

$\mathcal{O}$nce I was in a small country church when a little boy began to squirm and talk out loud. After several warnings, his father tucked him under his arm and walked up the aisle to take him out. As they reached the back of

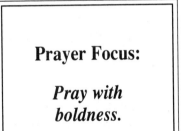

Prayer Focus:

Pray with boldness.

the auditorium, the boy said in a loud voice, "Y'all pray for me!"

He hadn't quite learned "church protocol," but he had learned something about prayer. We need to pray for others, but we also need their prayers. In his letters Paul gives thanks for the churches and prays God will grant them certain spiritual blessings. Because Paul does not think himself spiritually superior to his readers, he not only prays for them, he requests their prayers. In asking for their prayers, Paul is teaching them, and us, not only what to pray for, but that they can join together—with him and with others—to pray.

Request Prayer

Paul is not a spiritual loner. He knows his limitations and knows there are many who oppose the gospel. So he frequently asks his fellow Christians to support him through prayer.

> I urge you, brothers, by our Lord Jesus Christ and by the love of the Spirit, to join me in my struggle by praying to God for me. Pray that I may be rescued from the unbelievers in Judea and that my service in Jerusalem may be acceptable to the saints there, so that by God's will I may come to you with joy and together with you be refreshed. The God of peace be with you all. Amen (Romans 15:30-33).

Ask for Support

Two nagging concerns overshadowed Paul's coming trip to Jerusalem. One was the opposition he would face there. This was no figment of Paul's imagination. Already the unbelieving Jews had tried to kill him (Acts 9:29). Their hatred of Paul was understandable. To them he was a turncoat. Once he had stood firm for the Law and against these wayward Jews who were loyal to the Nazarene. But he had been deceived into following Jesus. Paul knew their hatred and their power, so he asked the support of the churches. He asked the Romans to pray for his deliverance that he might afterward come to visit them in Rome (Romans 15:32). Their prayer for Paul is answered, though not in the way Paul might have expected. He is indeed delivered from death in

Jerusalem, but he comes to Rome in chains, a prisoner of the unbelievers (Acts 21:27, 28, 31; 27:1).

This is not the only time that Paul faced danger from unbelievers. Everywhere he went, he made enemies. In Asia, he faced a severe trial that threatened to completely crush his spirit (2 Corinthians 1:8-11). But God rescued him, and he is confident God will save him again. Paul has this confidence through prayer. He asks the Corinthians as well as the Romans to "help us by your prayers" (2 Corinthians 1:11; see also Philippians 1:19; 2 Thessalonians 3:1, 2). Paul never faced opposition alone; through prayer his fellow Christians and his heavenly Father stood beside him.

Ask for Unity

Paul's second concern regarding his Judean trip seems less realistic. He worries that his ministry to the Jerusalem church (the gift of money he has collected from the Gentile churches) will not be accepted. Why would the Jerusalem Christians reject a gift for the poor, a gift they themselves had asked Paul to remember? Because this was no ordinary gift. It was a gift from predominantly Gentile churches to the Jewish church in Jerusalem. Paul intended for this gift to cement relations between Jews and Gentiles in the church since it demonstrated the love of Gentile Christians for their Jewish brothers and sisters. By receiving the gift, the Jerusalem church would be admitting that Gentiles are full heirs of Christ along with the Jews.

Don't forget that the Judaizers dogged Paul's every step. They refused to admit Gentiles into the church unless they first became Jews. These Judaizers were influential in the Jerusalem church, and it would not be out of character for them to let people starve rather than to compromise their principles to accept a gift from Gentiles. Paul then is actually asking the Romans to pray for unity among Christians. Their prayer was answered. The Jerusalem church warmly accepted Paul and the gift (Acts 21:17-20).

What do these requests for prayer say to us as Christians today? We also face opposition from unbelievers. They may not try to kill us, but they can insult, wound, and cause us to doubt. God will deliver us from such people when we pray. We sometimes struggle with disunity and bad feelings among Christians. Let us join in prayer for unity, so that the good gifts we have for one another will be warmly accepted. Then like Paul, we will never face opposition alone, because our Father and our church family are there standing beside us.

Ask for Boldness

When we are ridiculed for our Christian faith, our first reaction is to keep a low profile, to soft-pedal our Christianity or to keep completely quiet about it. Paul faced more than ridicule; he faced imprisonment, beatings, and death. But like us, Paul was only human and at times was tempted to be quiet about Christ. Facing that temptation, he asks the churches to pray for him.

Pray also for me, that whenever I open my mouth, words may be given me so that I will fearlessly make known the mystery of the gospel, for which I am an ambassador in chains. Pray that I may declare it fearlessly, as I should (Ephesians 6:19, 20).

Devote yourselves to prayer, being watchful and thankful. And pray for us, too, that God may open a door for our message, so that we may proclaim the mystery of Christ, for which I am in chains. Pray that I may proclaim it clearly, as I should (Colossians 4:2-4).

In these passages Paul asks for boldness to proclaim the mystery of the gospel. He knows opposition can make his witness timid. He knows how much easier it would be for him if he would soften the absolute teachings of the Christian message, so he prays he may reveal Christ clearly.

When we take our faith seriously, then we cannot help but tell others the good news.

The daily opposition we face from a hostile culture tempts us also to weaken our witness. We say, "Yes, I'm a Christian, but I don't condemn those who aren't" or "I believe the Bible, but if you don't, you're certainly entitled to your opinion" or "I don't want to force my beliefs on anyone." Or we say nothing at all. We are completely silent about our faith in the presence of unbelievers. But when we believe Jesus is who he says he is, and when we take our faith seriously, then we cannot help but tell others the good news. Christian witness is not optional. We either confess Christ or we don't. Confession is not just a onetime statement at our baptism. It's an ongoing process. When we fail to confess him, he will fail to confess us.

But where can we get the courage to confess Christ when it is embarrassing and may even cost us friendships, promotions, and acceptance? Only in prayer. If the bold apostle Paul needed to ask for courage and boldness, surely we need to ask. And we should pray for other Christians to be emboldened by God.

We were never meant to live our Christian lives

alone. Our prayer lives are not to be merely private. Like Paul we need at times to say, "Brothers, pray for us" (1 Thessalonians 5:25). It is only through the prayers of our brothers and sisters and the blessing of our heavenly Father that we can live the demanding life of a bold Christian.

Rejoice in Suffering

Paul knew the hardships and challenges the churches in Rome, Philippi, and Corinth were facing and would continue to face. So he writes to encourage them in their faith. His positive attitude and his faith in prayer send a message of strength and hope to the struggling early Christians. Through prayer, we, too, can receive the blessings of strength and hope in the face of suffering and anxiety.

Be Joyful

Paul tells the Romans, "Be joyful in hope, patient in affliction, faithful in prayer" (Romans 12:12). We must be persistent in prayer even in our darkest hours. The pressures of life sometimes threaten to overwhelm us. In our despair we may be tempted to stop praying, thinking, "What's the use?" But perseverance in prayer leads to patience in suffering, and no matter how bad things get, we can still rejoice in the hope of resurrection. Our suffering may even be fatal, but it is not final. God holds us in his hand.

Be Thankful

These two strange bedfellows—rejoicing and suffering—are found together in many New Testament passages. Paul urges the Philippians to rejoice and be thankful even in the midst of anxiety.

Rejoice in the Lord always. I will say it again:

Rejoice! Let your gentleness be evident to all. The Lord is near. Do not be anxious about anything, but in everything, by prayer and petition, with thanksgiving, present your requests to God. And the peace of God, which transcends all understanding, will guard your hearts and your minds in Christ Jesus (Philippians 4:4-7).

This is certainly one of the most reassuring scriptures in the Bible. Christian joy stems not from circumstances but from the realization that "the Lord is near." Paul encourages us by saying, "Don't worry, pray." Our lives produce great anxiety, but if we thankfully take our worries to God, he will give us peace that passes understanding.

The sure solution to worry, which these verses promise, is quite different from the prescriptions of our age. Paul does not urge us to think positively, to believe in ourselves, or to minimize the reasons for our worry. Dedicated Christians have good reason to be worried, after all, the world is against us. The peace we are promised is not the result of a twelve-step program or any particular technique. It is the free gift of God in prayer. It is a peace that passes understanding because it is not based on the pleasantness of our circumstances, but on our trusting faith in a Father who guards us.

Boast about Weaknesses

It is also a strange peace because even when we persist in prayer, God does not always relieve the cause of our anxiety. Paul knew this personally. When he speaks of pain and anxiety, he speaks not as a bystander, but as one who knew them intimately. He shares how he deals with his pain in his letter to the Corinthians:

> To keep me from becoming conceited because of
> these surpassingly great revelations, there was
> given me a thorn in my flesh, a messenger of
> Satan, to torment me. Three times I pleaded with
> the Lord to take it away from me. But he said to
> me, "My grace is sufficient for you, for my power
> is made perfect in weakness." Therefore I will
> boast all the more gladly about my weaknesses,
> so that Christ's power may rest on me. That is
> why, for Christ's sake, I delight in weaknesses, in
> insults, in hardships, in persecutions, in difficul-
> ties. For when I am weak, then I am strong
> (2 Corinthians 12:7-10).

Speculation on the exact nature of Paul's thorn in
the flesh is fruitless; whatever it may have been, it
certainly caused him pain and anxiety. He does not
blame God for the thorn (it is "a messenger of Satan"), but he does appeal to Jesus for relief. Notice if
you have a red-letter edition Bible that Jesus himself answers Paul's pleading: "My grace is sufficient
for you."

What kind of answer is this? Did Jesus not promise to heal our hurts and remove our worries? Yes.
And that is precisely what he does for Paul. He does
not remove the pain, but he makes it of no account.
He places it in a new perspective. "My grace is sufficient," Jesus says, "for my power is made perfect in
weakness." Jesus offers Paul more than healing; he
offers grace and perfection. The Lord did not send
the thorn, but he is so powerful he can take this evil
thing and use it for Paul's own good—and for God's
own good. Paul is not healed, but his anxiety is
taken away as his torment is swallowed up in the
grace of God. It is only in our weakness that there is
room for the presence of God to be evident in our

lives. Where there is no weakness, there is no place
for God's strength.

---

*Where there is no weakness,
there is no place for God's strength.*

Jesus' answer to Paul and his three prayers
reminds us that he, too, cried to God in pain. Like
Jesus in Gethsemane, Paul had a cross to bear. Like
Jesus, he trusted the will of the Father.

Jesus and Paul are not alone. Each Christian
must take up his own cross. We are called to suffer
with Jesus. He certainly promises us relief from pain
and anxiety, but he does not promise our sicknesses
will always be cured or our path always be made
smooth. In pain we cry to the Lord, and he hears us.
He may remove the pain, or he may say, "My grace
is enough, you must bear this cross." That answer
should be enough for us, for he suffers with us,
perfecting us in weakness and giving us a sure hope.

Pray in the Spirit

All this sounds marvelous, but can we really do
it? Can we really pray that God's will be done? Can
we be happy with God's answer if he chooses not to
heal our pain? What should we pray for? Healing?
Faith? Courage? Resignation? How do we know what
God's will is for us?

All of these questions point to one fact: when it
comes to prayer, we need help. The good news is: we
have it.

In the same way, the Spirit helps us in our weakness. We do not know what we ought to pray for,

but the Spirit himself intercedes for us with groans that words cannot express. And he who searches our hearts knows the mind of the Spirit, because the Spirit intercedes for the saints in accordance with God's will (Romans 8:26, 27).

"We do not know what we ought to pray for." Truer words were never spoken. Like the disciples, we must ask, "Lord, teach us to pray." But this passage deals less with the technique of prayer than with the content of prayer. Not only do we not know the right words to say, we do not even know what to pray for. We all have had loved ones on the verge of death. For what should we pray? For healing? Perhaps, for even if the doctors have given up hope, our God still holds life in his hands. But what if it is not God's will to heal them? Do we pray they face death with courage? Do we pray for a quick and painless death?

> *Praying in the Spirit is the rule, not the exception, of the Christian's prayer life.*

These are not hypothetical questions. We all have struggled with these situations. But we do not pray alone, the Spirit prays with us. He takes our stumbling words, our doubts, and our struggles, and he translates them into "sighs too deep for words." We don't always know how to speak to God, but the Spirit knows, and he speaks for us. Paul wanted his readers to know that the effectiveness of prayer depends not on our ability to speak or on the clarity of our desires, but on the power of the Spirit.

Praying in the Spirit is the rule, not the exception,

of the Christian's prayer life. Truly spiritual prayer
is not measured by how we feel, or how right we get
the words. We don't have to pray "good" to pray in
the Spirit. Even when we have no idea what to pray,
even when we don't want to pray, the Spirit is there
to help us. Yes, particularly when we just can't seem
to pray, when we are victims of our weakness, the
Spirit intercedes. He amplifies our groanings as
God's own megaphone. And God hears our cry.

So what should keep us from praying? Trouble?
No, we are to take our worries to God. Our sins? No,
for we rely on God's grace in prayer. Our own inepti-
tude? No, for the Spirit speaks for us. When we pray
in the Spirit all the time (Ephesians 6:18), then our
prayers are always adequate, even when we are not.

Learn from Paul

Through Paul's letters to the churches, we get to
know Paul and his heart for prayer. Through these
prayers we find powerful motivation to:

Pray regularly. First, we see Paul, like Jesus,
constant in prayer. We, too, should make prayer a
regular part of our lives. Prayer is not just for
churchtime, mealtime, or bedtime. All of these are
appropriate times for prayer. But for prayer to
provide the gift God desires for us, these "routine"
times must not be the sum of our prayer life. Prayer
is for all times and anytime.

Pray for others. Paul prayed for others. The
biblical word for this is *intercession*. Other Christians desperately need our prayers, and we need
theirs. Paul realized he needed the prayers of the
churches, so he asked for them. When trouble comes,
we are not expected merely to grin and bear it; we
are to pray and wait for God's answer. He never

wants us to bear our burdens alone—others help carry them to God. In Christ, we are all in this battle together—others' troubles become ours and then we give them to him. Nothing revitalizes churches more than a commitment to pray for one another and ask one another for prayer.

Pray for spiritual blessings. Paul's requests to God for the churches, and the causes of his thankfulness to God are usually spiritual matters. He rarely thanks God for their health or wealth, but he is thankful for their faith, hope, and love. He seldom asks God to bless them with the ordinary blessings of life, but he does pray God to give them spiritual discernment, steadfastness, and power. It certainly is not wrong to ask for health or daily bread, but Paul knew what was of real value. When we pray for ourselves or others, we must also ask God for everlasting blessings—the spiritual gifts—for only they will last into the coming kingdom.

Encourage others. Finally, it is significant that Paul told his readers that he was praying for them. In those rough weeks when everything goes wrong, our faith is tested, and we hover on the edge of despair, how marvelous it is to hear someone say, "I am praying for you." We should not only pray for our brothers and sisters in Christ, we should encourage them by telling them how thankful we are to God for them and how we have asked his blessing to be on them.

Pray with power. Paul says we don't pray as we should. Thank God that his power doesn't depend on the correctness of our prayers. The effectiveness of our prayers is not dependent upon our own abilities. Regardless of our personal weaknesses and "thorns" we have to contend with, we hold the unlimited power that comes with being devoted believers. We have a helper: the Holy Spirit. He intercedes for us, translating our pitiful attempts at expression into words beyond words that touch the heart of the Father. Whenever we pray sincerely and in faith, we pray with power.

So the heart of Christian prayer is this: prayer is from beginning to end a work of God. God the Father is the object of prayer—the powerful, loving one to whom we pray. God the Son is our model and companion in prayer; we pray in his name, and he prays with us. God the Spirit is our helper in prayer, turning our words into God's words.

This takes the pressure off us in prayer. While we may not fully understand how God wants us to pray, we can still confidently say like the little boy in church, "Ya'll pray for me." Because we never pray alone. We have all the help we need—help that allows us to pray with boldness and to rejoice in that boldness!

Focusing Your Faith:

1. How do you generally respond when things don't go your way or you're really anxious about something? What message does that send to those around you?

2. What person can you most easily turn to for help when you are really struggling? Have you ever asked this person to pray for you?

3. The Jews in the Jerusalem church refused to accept the Gentiles into the church until they became Jews, and Paul feared they would reject their money. Whom have you "rejected" because they didn't conform to your standards?

4. When have you been forced to be "quiet about Christ"? When have you been bold for Christ?

5. How can you witness Christ to others without trying to "straighten them out"?

6. How can you tell when the Spirit is working in you?

7. What thorn has Satan given you to torment you? How has God blessed you because of it?

Part 4:

PRAYERS OF FAITH AND DISCIPLINE

Chapter 11

The Power
of Faith

$\mathcal{T}$olstoy told the story of three simple hermit monks who lived on an island. It seems that great things happened when they prayed this simple prayer: "We are three; you are three; have mercy on us. Amen."

Prayer Focus:

Pray with assurance.

Hearing of these hermits, the bishop decided they needed guidance and instruction on prayer. So he sailed to the island and instructed them on the proper methods of prayer.

As the bishop was sailing back to the mainland, he suddenly saw the three hermits running across the water to him in a great ball of light. When they reached the ship, they asked the bishop, "We're sorry, but we've forgotten some of your teachings. Could you please tell us again?"

The bishop humbly replied, "Forget everything I've taught you. Continue to pray as usual."

Sometimes we make prayer more difficult and complex than it really is. Prayers of faith, no matter how simple, can be very powerful.

The Gospels, Acts, and Paul's letters are not the only New Testament books to mention prayer. Indeed, almost every New Testament book discusses prayer, showing how central prayer is to the life of the disciples. Throughout the New Testament the same prayer themes are developed and emphasized by the various authors. Two books that give us new insights into prayer are Hebrews and James. They teach us the importance of faith in the believer's prayer.

Prayer in Hebrews

Hebrews is an unusual book. We are not sure who wrote it or who originally received it. It does not read like a letter or a history or a Gospel. Most scholars now believe Hebrews is a written sermon, since the author himself calls it a brief word of exhortation (Hebrews 13:22). To contemporary Christians it must seem like a strange sermon. It certainly is not brief by our modern standards. It contains detailed arguments and obscure terminology from Old Testament sacrificial passages that modern audiences find difficult, if not downright impossible, to follow.

Grace through Faith

In spite of its strangeness to the modern mind, Hebrews is a book to be treasured by contemporary Christians. The writer of Hebrews displays the superiority and finality of Jesus, and he urges his readers to be faithful to the pioneer of their salvation. In his reflection on the superiority of Jesus' high priesthood, he remembers the prayers in the garden of Gethsemane: "During the days of Jesus' life on earth, he offered up prayers and petitions with loud cries and tears to the one who could save him from death, and he was heard because of his reverent submission" (Hebrews 5:7).

In the garden, with loud cries and tears, Jesus begged the Father to save him from death, yet he prayed, "Your will be done."

> *To have our prayer heard means to have it answered, to receive God's blessing.*

When we read the Gospel accounts of Jesus in Gethsemane, it may seem God did not hear Jesus' prayer; after all, he still had to go to the cross. According to Hebrews, God heard Jesus' prayer in the garden. But in what sense did God hear his prayer? Does this simply mean God heard him but said no to his request? I don't think so. To have our prayer heard means to have it answered, to receive God's blessing. The Hebrew writer contends God granted Jesus' prayer to be saved from death—through resurrection. Not only that, through his obedience he was made perfect. God declared him our eternal high priest and the source of our salvation (Hebrews 5:8-10).

Perhaps, like me, you've heard that God answers prayer one of three ways: yes, no, and not yet. This passage from Hebrews makes it clear that God has only one answer. When we ask in faith, and ask in the will of God as Jesus did in the garden, then God always answers yes. That yes, however, may take a form beyond our wildest dreams: resurrection, new life, new self.

There is an important lesson here for us. God does not always give us what we want or think we need, but he always hears us and gives us something better than what we request. We may ask for relief from pain, for comfort for our broken hearts, for ease for our tired souls. He may not give us these. His answer may be, "My grace is sufficient for you" or "You must bear your cross." But he has a greater gift for us: the gift of resurrection, of new life. When we pray as Christians, we don't pray with shallow optimism that things will immediately get better, but we pray with confident hope. We know that God hears us and will bless in his own way and time. Like Jesus in the garden, we may have to learn obedience through suffering. But like him we can trust our loving Father who holds life in his hands and who answers our prayers.

It's not only by grace that we are saved, it's by grace that we pray.

By learning obedience, Jesus became our great high priest, the one who takes our sins to the Father.

> Now there have been many of those priests, since death prevented them from continuing in office; but because Jesus lives forever, he has a permanent priesthood. Therefore he is able to save completely those who come to God through him, because he always lives to intercede for them (Hebrews 7:23-25).

Jesus is our priest forever; he saves us for all

time. Old Testament priests offered sacrifices to cover the people's sins. Jesus offered himself for us once for all (Hebrews 7:27). As both our sacrifice and our priest, he lives to make intercession for us.

Why do we need intercession? Don't we have a heavenly Father who loves us and listens to us? Yes, but our sins have torn us away from the Father, blocking our path to the Most Holy God. But our Savior intercedes for us in prayer. He removes our sin, makes us right with God, and makes our requests for us. We can approach God boldly, for when we pray, Christ, our priest and sacrifice, prays with us. Our prayers become his prayers to the Father. He lives to pray for us. It's not only by grace that we are saved, it's by grace that we pray.

Plea for Unity

Another reference to prayer in Hebrews sounds quite familiar: "Pray for us. We are sure that we have a clear conscience and desire to live honorably in every way. I particularly urge you to pray so that I may be restored to you soon" (Hebrews 13:18, 19).

As we saw with Paul, no Christian is so mature that he can afford to do without the prayers of fellow Christians. The Hebrew writer, like Paul, particularly asks his readers to pray that he may see them soon. This is an intriguing phrase. Has there been bad blood between the writer and his readers? Is that why he indicates that he has a clear conscience? What has prevented him from going to them? Imprisonment? Sickness? Their own attitude? His work in other ministries? We are not told, but we do know he now wants to see them, and he asks them to pray that he will.

Nothing should separate Christian brothers and sisters. Too many times we allow things to come between us and fellow Christians. Perhaps an inappropriate word was said, perhaps we felt ignored or ridiculed, perhaps we simply grew distant from neglect. From Hebrews we learn that the barriers existing between Christians must be torn away by prayer. We must pray and ask our fellow Christians to pray that we will be restored to each other soon.

Prayer in James

The author of James, probably Jesus' brother, was the leader of the Jerusalem Council. Paul called him a pillar of the church. It is no surprise then that James's writing reflects many of Jesus' teachings, especially those from the Sermon on the Mount.

Faith through Wisdom

James is full of practical advice for Christians, and so we would expect him to teach on prayer. At the very beginning of his book, after urging his readers to find joy even in trials, he tells them to ask for wisdom:

> If any of you lacks wisdom, he should ask God, who gives generously to all without finding fault, and it will be given to him. But when he asks, he must believe and not doubt, because he who doubts is like a wave of the sea, blown and tossed by the wind. That man should not think he will receive anything from the Lord; he is a double-minded man, unstable in all he does (James 1:5-8).

Although the word "prayer" does not occur in this passage, we discover how to ask God for what we need. We are told to ask for wisdom—something we need and God wants to give us. We particularly need wisdom to see our daily trials as opportunities to strengthen our faith. And we can pray in confidence, knowing the God to whom we pray is generous and will give us the wisdom we need.

Wisdom through Faith

Yet this receiving of wisdom is no automatic transaction. James warns us to be careful how we ask for it. Our petitions to God must not be half-hearted; we cannot be in two minds as to whether God will bless. God is good. God is great. He will give us what we need. All that prevents him from doing so are our own doubts. James is not questioning God's power to give, but rather our power to receive. How in the world can we expect to get wisdom from God if we are foolish enough to doubt him? James echoes the words of Jesus, ". . . have faith and do not doubt" (Matthew 21:21).

God is great. He will give us
what we need. All that prevents him
from doing so are our own doubts.

Doubt is not the only hindrance to prayer. Conflict, apathy, and selfishness also block our way to God.

What causes fights and quarrels among you? Don't they come from your desires that battle within you? You want something but don't get it. You kill and covet, but you cannot have what you want. You quarrel and fight. You do not have, because you do not ask God. When you ask, you do not receive, because you ask with wrong motives, that you may spend what you get on your plea-sures (James 4:1-3).

Why is it we don't get what we want from God?
One reason, James says, is we don't ask. Why don't
we always ask God for what we want? We may
realize what we want is not what we really need. Or
perhaps we doubt God's power or desire to help us.
Maybe we think we can get what we want without
his help; self-sufficiency gets in the way of prayer. It
is not as though God needs us to ask before he can
bless—he already knows what we need. But for our
own sake, we need to ask. We need to be reminded of
our dependence on our Father.

Will God give us everything we ask for? No. Not if
we ask selfishly for what brings pleasure only to us.
God is not a genie in a bottle who grants our wishes.
Prayer is not a magical formula for wealth or pleasure. When we pray we must be careful to ask for
what is ultimately good and pleasurable, not for
immediate gratification of our desires. We don't
want to be like the youngster in Sunday school
having a great time making greeting cards for the
sick and shut-ins. He prayed for more sick people so
he could make more cards. Instead, we should pray
with the needs and wants of others in mind, not just
for what we want or what is best for us.

Power in God's Will

God will give us wisdom and everything else we
need, but not necessarily everything we want. He
always answers our prayers, but we must sometimes
wait for his answer. However, the need for trust and
patience does not mean prayer does not work. James
assures us that prayer is powerful:

> Is any one of you in trouble? He should pray. Is
> anyone happy? Let him sing songs of praise. Is
> any one of you sick? He should call the elders of

the church to pray over him and anoint him with oil in the name of the Lord. And the prayer offered in faith will make the sick person well; the Lord will raise him up. If he has sinned, he will be forgiven. Therefore confess your sins to each other and pray for each other so that you may be healed. The prayer of a righteous man is powerful and effective.

Elijah was a man just like us. He prayed earnestly that it would not rain, and it did not rain on the land for three and a half years. Again he prayed, and the heavens gave rain, and the earth produced its crops (James 5:13-18).

James lists all the marvelous things God will do for us when we confess our sins to each other and pray for each other. He will help us in times of trouble, heal our sickness, and forgive our sins. Prayer to God is, beyond a doubt, "powerful and effective." Elijah prayed for drought and then for rain as a sign to the Israelites (1 Kings 17:1; 18:1), and God answered his prayers immediately because they were in accordance with his will. We can pray with the same fervor and assurance, knowing our prayers are effective when we pray in God's will.

God is not in our power, we are in his. Our prayers reflect the whole of our life of obedience to him. They flow from our faith and our acts of service. All of life is our prayer to God—an expression of our faith in him. Working, playing, serving, teaching, singing, studying, caring—all are prayers when done to his glory.

When we keep our minds focused on God in prayer, he energizes our spiritual lives. Prayer is not just a righteous act—prayer is a gift. It is the gift to us who are made righteous by the blood of Christ.

Focusing Your Faith:

1. Which comes first, faith or wisdom?

2. Do you really believe God will make you wise? Ask for wisdom in prayer.

3. How did suffering to the point of death give Jesus insights into obedience?

4. What comfort do you feel knowing Jesus is your high priest? How does his priesthood give you confidence in coming to God?

5. How have you learned obedience through suffering? What did God teach you?

6. What lesson has God taught you about patience? How long did you have to wait for your answer?

7. Think of some ways your church can use prayer to bring about peace and unity in your local congregation.

Chapter 12

No-Pain-No-Gain
Spirituality

$\mathcal{I}$n a time when families are pulled in many directions, discipline is a practice that often falls by the wayside. Susanna Wesley, wife of a minister and mother of nineteen children, has gone down in Christian history as

> **Prayer Focus:**
>
> *Pray with discipline.*

an ideal mother. In spite of poverty, sickness, and disappointment, she managed her household with strength.

Some of her disciplinary rules included: (1) No child was to be given a thing because he cried for it. If a child wanted to cry, he must cry softly; (2) There would be no eating and drinking between meals, except when sick; (3) Each one must eat and drink everything before him; (4) Sleeping was regulated. When very small, a child would be allowed three hours sleep in the morning and three in the afternoon. This was shortened until no sleeping would be allowed during the daytime; (5) The little ones were placed in the cradle and rocked to sleep. At 7:00 PM, each child was to be put to bed; at 8:00 PM Mrs. Wesley left the room. She never allowed herself to sit by the bed until the child slept; (6) Children must address each other as "Sister____" or "Brother____." Susanna Wesley's form of discipline might be labeled "rigid" or even "abusive" nowadays, but at least two of her children—John and Charles—turned out to be well-known ministers.

Discipline is almost a bad word today. We live in an age of freedom, of excess, of feeling good about ourselves. *Discipline* conjures up images of monks in their cells, marines on Parris Island, or the worst of reform schools. The only place we seem to meet discipline today is in the gym. Many are almost religious about their workouts. "No pain, no gain," they say. But the discipline Peter and John urge us to have is a discipline of prayer. In their books they explore the place of prayer in the lives of obedient disciples, clearly revealing prayer's power and beauty.

Prayer in 1 Peter

Peter writes to "the exiles of the Dispersion" (NRSV), Jewish and Gentile Christians scattered throughout Asia Minor, to encourage them to be faithful even though they must suffer as Jesus did. "Exiles" is a significant term. It implies these Christians had been torn not only physically from Jerusalem, but also from the prevailing social structure that had been the center of their lives, because of their faith in Christ. Now they were citizens of a new holy kingdom and their old companions, surprised at their new behavior, ostracized and even persecuted them. Still they continued to persist in the course they had set—to follow Jesus. Certainly this situation was one for prayer.

Prayer in Marriage

Peter speaks of prayer in this letter in relation to husbands and wives. He instructs his readers on Christian marriage, telling wives to accept the authority of their husbands and telling husbands to show consideration for their wives. Following this instruction would, no doubt, promote harmony in the home and set a good example for those outside the church. But these are not the primary purposes Peter gives for his advice. Instead, wives and husbands are to act this way "so that nothing will hinder your prayers" (1 Peter 3:7).

Peter draws a connection between the health of the marriage relationship and the degree to which our prayers are heard by God and are carried to him unhindered. Likewise, there is a relationship between the effectiveness of our prayer life and how we treat our partners.

This is the only New Testament reference to prayer in marriage (except, perhaps, for 1 Corinthians 7:5). But its offhanded tone implies that shared prayer between spouses was taken for granted by early Christians. Trouble between Christian marriage partners is particularly disturbing because it gets in the way of their prayers. Here Peter advises husbands that the way they treat their wives influences whether or not their prayers are accepted. In our modern world, not sleeping together is often the sign of marital difficulty. To Peter, not being able to pray together is even more devastating to the relationship.

The plight of the American family is on everyone's

mind these days. Countless seminars, retreats, and books are out there, telling us how to save our marriages and families. No doubt they do some good. But no marriage can be saved, no family strengthened without the discipline and power of prayer. It's such a cliché, but it's still true: The family that prays together, stays together.

> *No marriage can be saved,*
> *no family strengthened without the*
> *discipline and power of prayer.*

Jesus and Paul, among others, taught and modeled the need for Christians—even those who were not well-acquainted and those who were quarreling—to pray for and with each other. How much more important is it for those who are married to pray together? But how often do we pray with those who are dearest to us—our husband, our wife, our children? Are we too busy? Do we consider prayer purely a private affair, none of our family's business? Peter will not allow that. He expects his readers to pray together. When we take the Bible seriously, we can pursue prayer passionately, making prayer an integral and central part of our lives.

Prayer in the Last Days

Peter also places prayer in the context of the end of the world: "The end of all things is near; therefore be serious and discipline yourselves for the sake of your prayers" (1 Peter 4:7, NRSV). Christians live in the shadow of the cross and in anticipation of the return of Christ. Many Christians today seem to think little about the end of the world. Even when they do, too much attention is given to idle speculation about the signs of the times. We do not know when he will return, but we are to believe he will. Each generation of Christians lives in the last days. Each can say, "Jesus is coming soon."

When we are convinced his coming is near, our prayer life is changed. Our prayer life becomes something serious, something that should not be played at, but that should be nurtured in a controlled way. Peter's word is "discipline" (NRSV) or "self-control" (NIV). He reminds us there is something more important than the health and strength of our bodies, more important than anything in this world. The end of all things is near. That realization should motivate us to be clear-minded and disciplined in prayer. Soon all that will be left is the reality of the God to whom we pray. With that in mind, we would do well to dedicate more attention to our spiritual discipline than our physical workouts.

Wrestling with God in prayer can be painful, but as with all discipline, no pain, no gain.

Discipline in prayer means to pray regularly, even when we don't feel like it, even when it is not convenient, even when it hurts. Just do it. Wrestling with God in prayer can be painful, but as with all discipline, no pain, no gain.

Prayer in John's Letters

One purpose of John's letters was to give believers an assurance of salvation. For the Christian who is clothed with the righteousness of Christ, there is also an assurance that God answers prayer. When

John speaks of prayer, he repeats a theme found
throughout the New Testament—ask and you will
receive. "Dear friends, if our hearts do not condemn
us, we have confidence before God and receive from
him anything we ask, because we obey his commands and do what pleases him" (1 John 3:21, 22).

John's words are similar to the words of Jesus ("If
you believe, you will receive whatever you ask for in
prayer" Matthew 21:22), and to the advice of James
("But when he asks, he must believe and not doubt,
because he who doubts is like a wave of the sea,
blown and tossed by the wind" James 1:6). To John,
however, the confidence that we will receive what we
ask from God is based not only on faith, but also on
obedience. John is not advocating a "works righteousness" of demanding perfection from Christians, but
he, like James, teaches that faith and obedience are
inseparable. True faith leads to obedience, and to
obey God is to "believe in the name of his Son, Jesus
Christ, and to love one another as he commanded us"
(1 John 3:23). John goes on to say that those who
obey Jesus' commands live in him and that he lives
in them. How do we know that he lives in us? We
know it by the Spirit he gave us—the same Spirit
that helps us pray (verse 24).

John understands the relationship between moral
and ethical purity and our surrender to the reign of
God. When we allow God's will to reign in our hearts,
we will be disciplined in our prayers, and God's
power will be unleashed in our lives. In other words,
prayer is part of something much larger—our entire
relationship to God. It is legitimate and right to ask
God for what we need, but when we approach him
we should not be a stranger to him. We don't have to
wait to pray only when we are desperate or have
exhausted our own resources or when we, quite

frankly, have nothing better to do. We can pray to our Father, and as a devoted Father, he gives us what we ask. Such a Father deserves and lovingly demands our trust and obedience. It is when "our hearts do not condemn us," when we know our relationship to our Father is genuine, when Jesus lives in us and we in him, that we can approach him boldly.

When we allow God's will to reign in our hearts, we will be disciplined in our prayers, and God's power will be unleashed in our lives.

In his closing remarks, John tells us that we can know we have eternal life and that this knowledge causes us to approach God with confidence.

> I write these things to you who believe in the name of the Son of God so that you may know that you have eternal life. This is the confidence we have in approaching God: that if we ask anything according to his will, he hears us. And if we know that he hears us—whatever we ask—we know that we have what we asked of him (1 John 5:13-15).

Sin is a little-used word in our society, even in the church. In America we believe strongly in the individual's freedom to do whatever he or she wants, "as long as it doesn't hurt anyone." As part of a church, many Christians feel they should mind their own business, saying Christianity is a purely private affair and the foibles of their fellow Christians are strictly between them and God. But John disagrees:

If anyone sees his brother commit a sin that does not lead to death, he should pray and God will give him life. I refer to those whose sin does not lead to death. There is a sin that leads to death. I am not saying that he should pray about that. All wrongdoing is sin, and there is sin that does not lead to death (1 John 5:16, 17).

Satan deceives us, lulling us into a false sense of security when we think we can enjoy the luxury of a strictly private Christianity. We are privileged to be responsible for each other, whether we understand it now or not. Your sins, even when they are not personally against me, are my concern, for you are my brother or sister. Oh yes, my sins are your concern too.

A Christ-minded church can overcome Satan's temptation to become a bunch of busybodies, eager to find the latest dirt on others. On the contrary, my love for Christ empowers me with concern for your sins. Because of my love for him, I will never use them against you or belittle you, but I will hide your sins completely by asking God to forgive them. And when you see me sin, you, too, are to pray for my forgiveness with the same mercy and compassion of Christ.

I'm not completely sure what John means about a sin that leads to death that should not be prayed for; perhaps any sin that we refuse to acknowledge can become a mortal sin. But John clearly challenges us modern Christians to honestly confess our sins and take responsibility for our brothers and sisters. Too many times in church we put up a false front. Sure, we admit we are sinners (isn't everyone?), but the last thing we would do is to confess a particular sin.

We are not called to wallow in our sins or to

graphically depict our every evil action, but we are expected to confess our sins. How much easier it is to lovingly confront other Christians with their sins and to pray for and with them when we have first allowed them to know about and pray for our sins. We may not relish those confessions or confrontations, but because we are God's children, faithful in our service and clear-minded and disciplined in our prayers, we will pray for our fellow sinners and accept, even welcome, their prayers for us.

Prayer in Revelation

Dragons, beasts with scorpion's tails, plagues on horseback, and jeweled cities—what a magnificent, dramatic setting for a lesson on Christian living! In Revelation, the final book of the New Testament, we have a most beautiful and powerful picture of prayer. It reveals to us that while God will shake the creation in mighty ways, it is through prayer that God changes things.

Another angel, who had a golden censer, came and stood at the altar. He was given much incense to offer, with the prayers of all the saints, on the golden altar before the throne. The smoke of the incense, together with the prayers of the saints, went up before God from the angel's hand. Then the angel took the censer, filled it with fire from the altar, and hurled it on the earth; and there came peals of thunder, rumblings, flashes of lightning and an earthquake (Revelation 8:3-5).

As the Jews in the Old Testament offered incense to God in the temple, so we worship God in prayer. Our prayers go up to God as pleasing incense. He gladly receives the prayers of the saints.

It is appropriate that this is the final word of the New Testament on prayer. Prayer is sublime not because it has some inherent power or because we have the ability to pray beautifully. Prayer is sublime because the Lord God almighty desires our prayers, hears our prayers, and generously blesses. It is not the scent of our offerings that counts, but the glory of the One who receives them.

————❖————

For thine is the kingdom, and the power,
and the glory, for ever!
Amen.

Focusing Your Faith:

1. How would you rate the level of discipline in your household growing up? Your household now?

2. How do you recognize a spiritually mature Christian? A spiritually mature church?

3. If you knew Christ would return next Sunday, what would you do differently this week?

4. How much time weekly do you spend interacting with your family? Watching television? Staying physically fit? Reading the Bible? Praying?

5. Whom do you feel most comfortable confessing your sins to? Why? Would anyone feel comfortable confessing their sins to you? Why?

6. What is the goal of your prayer life?

7. Take a positive step in planning your week. In a daily planner, schedule time for prayer, family, work, worship services, and Bible study. Then add extra church activities and other appointments as time allows.